BILL WENNINGTON'S

TALES FROM

THE BULLS

HARDWOOD

Bill Wennington
with Kent McDill

SP
SPORTS
PUBLISHING
L.L.C.

www.SportsPublishingLLC.com

ISBN: 1-58261-792-9

Publisher: Peter L. Bannon
Senior managing editor: Susan M. Moyer
Acquisitions editor: Scott Musgrave
Developmental editor: Dean Miller
Art director: K. Jeffrey Higgerson
Dust jacket design: Kenneth J. O'Brien
Project manager: Alicia Wentworth
Imaging: Dustin Hubbart
Photo editor: Erin Linden-Levy
Vice president of sales and marketing: Kevin King
Media and promotions managers: Michael Hagan (regional),
    Randy Fouts (national), Maurey Williamson (print)

Printed in the United States of America

Sports Publishing L.L.C.
804 North Neil Street
Champaign, IL 61820

Phone: 1-877-424-2665
Fax: 217-363-2073
Web site: www.SportsPublishingLLC.com

I would like to thank the Chicago Bulls for the opportunity to play basketball for a great city and fantastic fans. Also, I would like to thank all the coaches who made me the player I became—Bernie Buckley, Jack Donohue, Lou Carnesecca, Dick Motta, Ettore Messina, Phil Jackson, and especially my high school coach, Bob McKillop, who really molded me into the player I could be. My dad Bill Sr. for starting me off with basketball in Canada (early morning practices, I have never been a morning person). Anita and Isadore Caputo, my in-laws, for helping me to understand values of all people, not just my own. My wife, Anne, for being there for me my whole career, always helping me to be a better player and man. I love you, Anne, my forever princess. My son, Robbie, for sharing me with everyone who invades his time with dad and understanding. I love you, Rob, you are my joy. My mom, Elswyth and Gary Harrison, who were always a call away with support and great advice. Hey Old Woman, I miss you!

—Bill Wennington

I dedicate this book to my mother, Marilyn McDill, who taught me how to enjoy life, and to the memory of my father, K.B. McDill, who taught me how to deal with it.

—Kent McDill

Contents

Acknowledgments

Kent McDill is a wonderful writer. He was really able to grasp my thoughts and rambling statements, and put them onto paper so that many could understand. He was also there for pretty much all of the hoopla, and he jogged my memory a lot. He also is a much better researcher than I am. Thanks Kent!

Then there is Anne. She has been very instrumental in my whole career. I believe that all people make their own futures, but with Anne's help, I believe my past and future couldn't be any better. Anne, you are the best! Grow old with me; the best is yet to be!

—Bill Wennington

I want to thank Bill Wennington for his time and his effort in pulling this together. His enthusiasm for the project never wavered, and he obviously did a great job of capsulizing the personalities that made the story of the Bulls' championships such a compelling one.

I would like to acknowledge Roland Lazenby's book Blood on the Horns, which told in great detail the story of the Bulls in the 1997-98 season. Bill and I went through it to see what stories needed to be told from an insider's perspective.

I want to thank the Daily Herald for allowing me to cover the Bulls from 1988 through the 1999 season. The newspaper spared no expense in covering that remarkable story.

Thank you to the Chicago Bulls and their media department for all their help over the years.

Thank you also to my family; my wife, Janice, and the kids—Haley, Dan, Lindsey and Kyle. I spent a lot of time on the book that might have been spent with you, and I thank you for giving me that time.

—Kent McDill

Introduction

After my first six years in the NBA, I reached the summer of 1993. I had finished my second year playing in Italy, where the money was good and the opportunity was great.

My contract was over, and I wanted to give the NBA one more chance, because I knew I could play and produce.

The only two teams that showed any interest in me, because I had been gone for two years, were Portland and the Bulls. I went to summer camp with Portland, but the Trail Blazers eventually signed Chris Dudley, and they had another young kid they were grooming for the center position. The Bulls had people seeing me play in the summer league, and they contacted my agent.

The Bulls guaranteed me one month with the team, and I thought I would play enough that it would inspire another team to pick me up. If not, in December, the foreign teams would start looking at NBA players that had been cut, and I could go back there.

I saw Michael Jordan in that first Bulls camp. He and I had played together in the McDonald's All-American High School game in 1981, and he said he was excited to finally have a chance to play with me. And he winked at me. I didn't know why, but then two days later he retired.

I thought, oh well, I guess that is not going to happen.

Halfway through training camp, Scott Williams tore his anterior cruciate ligament.

The Bulls thought I was playing well, but they had four centers. One of them was Bill Cartwright, and because of his age, they didn't want him to have to play a lot in training camp.

So they decided to keep me another month, bring Bill along slowly, and then cut me.

But Bill didn't actually play until midseason, and all of a sudden, there was a position for me, along with Will Perdue and Stacey King.

On that early west coast trip of 1993, I had only played maybe 11 or 12 minutes in five games, and we were playing in Houston. We needed someone to play against Hakeem Olajuwon, and it turned out to be Will Perdue. I played maybe two minutes in the first half, and we were getting killed, down by about 20 points at halftime. Will got into foul trouble early in the third quarter, and Phil Jackson called me up and told me he was putting me into the game. "I'm sorry you are not prepared for this," he said. "All I want is for you not to get in foul trouble."

Well, I scored 16 points in the second half, had 12 or 13 rebounds, and we lost by two. Reporters called me Air Wennington after that game. It was an eye-opener for Phil, seeing that I could play and do the job. I started earning playing time from then on.

I think it is safe to say that coming to the Bulls as opposed to taking the shot with Portland turned out to be one of the best decisions of my life. Financially, I was given a lot more opportunity, and I am a lot more popular because I was on the Chicago Bulls team. I made a home in Chicago because I was on that team. I've been endeared to the Chicago sports fan because I was part of one of the best teams ever.

You can ask Charles Barkley and Patrick Ewing if they had great careers, and they will say yes, and they did. But if you ask them if they regret anything, they will say yes. They regret they didn't win a championship. Every team in the NBA has one great player that scores 21 points a night, but at the end of the year, there is only one team, and only 15 guys who will be NBA champions.

I ended up with three world championship rings, teammates and friends I will have for the rest of my life, a new home to raise my family, and a long list of stories to tell, ones people actually want to hear.

These are those stories.

CHAPTER ONE

Michael

None of this would have happened without Michael Jordan. None of the winning, none of the championships, not this book, and none of the many wonderful things that have happened in my life from the moment he rejoined the Bulls in 1995. If there are chapters in this book where Michael is not named, it is merely an oversight. Michael was the heartbeat that made the championship Chicago Bulls live.

Michael Jordan became the greatest basketball player in the history of the game not only because of his God-given physical skills, but also because of the way he developed those skills. There have been so many superlatives used to describe his abilities and his work ethic, new words had to be invented.

It is true the Bulls would not have won anything without Michael Jordan's talents. But the Bulls would not have won anything if Jordan had not pushed us all to be the best athletes we could be. It was his drive to win, and his drive to play with quality teammates, that made us into the team we were.

Michael Jordan believed that if you were in the NBA, you were there for a reason. He believed you had a talent, and you would work hard to get the most out of that talent. But he also believed that talent and hard work were only the beginning of the battle. You still had to prove your worth to him every day and you had to get better every day. He expected you in practice every day to be the best you could be. There were no days off with Michael Jordan around.

When we practiced, Michael expected you to have your shoes laced and be ready to play when you walked on the practice floor. That, in Michael's eyes, was a matter of professionalism. While Phil Jackson was our coach and the chief of our tribe, Michael was the leader. He was the brave who enforced the chief's rules. You had to have a system and a pecking order, and it went down from Michael.

Sometimes it was Phil who decided we could use a day off, and sometimes it was Michael who decided. We didn't ask who was responsible. But we knew no day off came without Michael agreeing to it.

Michael expected you to do your job every time you went on the court, whether it was for a game, a practice, or a shoot-around. I know every teammate had a way to tell when he had pleased or displeased Michael.

In my case, Michael would accept the fact that Shaquille O'Neal weighed 70 pounds more than I did or was two inches taller than I was. If Shaq ran over me, that was all right with Michael. He did not accept the fact that I might get out of Shaq's way because I didn't want to get hit. Michael had arguments with players all the time because their desire to play well and play hard did not live up to the expectations he had for them.

Michael Jordan made it all happen. (AP/WWP)

On the Nose

I remember a game in which Michael got mad at Luc Longley, our affable Australian center, because Luc wasn't focusing on catching the ball. Michael got tired of Luc's mishandling the ball, and he just refused to pass Luc the ball anymore.

With the triangle offense, when the ball is supposed to go somewhere, and it doesn't go there, everybody else is out of position. Phil (Jackson) called a time out and said, "Michael, you have to pass Luc the ball." But Michael wouldn't do it. He said, "No, I am not. I passed the ball to him twice, and he didn't catch it. I am not going to pass the ball to someone who is not going to catch the ball."

The next day in practice, we had a meeting, and Phil said it again. "Michael, you have to pass Luc the ball."

"Michael, I am trying my hardest," Luc said.

"Luc, you are not," Michael said in response. "You are not catching the ball. If I pass you the ball, you have to catch the ball."

They talked it out, had a good discussion, there was nothing heated, and Michael finally said, "Luc, I am going to pass you the ball in the next game, but if you don't catch it, it is going to break your nose." The next game, Michael passed the ball, hard and right at Luc's face. Luc caught it right in front of his nose. But he did catch it.

If Michael said something, he did it. And he expects you to respond in a certain way, all of it with the intention of playing the game of basketball at its highest level.

Does this all sound hard to believe? Well, it was all true. Like I said, superlatives do not do justice to the amount of drive Michael Jordan had to win. He knew he needed us to help him do it, and none of us was going to hold him back by playing to less than the best of our ability.

Motivational Ploy

Michael already had the greatest personal drive I have ever seen. But he then found a way to create within himself a greater desire to succeed. Michael would use different outside influences to motivate himself every day.

He hated seeing players sit out of practice, unless he saw a bone coming out of a key body part. He called guys out on our team, and got angry at them as a way to motivate himself. He would pull Ron Harper or Toni Kukoc into practice, even when they were sitting out with minor injuries. He would tell them, "We need you out there, you are part of the team." Then he would run right at them in practice.

You had to stand up to Michael, and you had to show him that your level of desire was at least in the same neighborhood as his. Then, of course, you ended up paying the price.

One day, early in practice, we were in a scrimmage. I was on the second team, Michael was on the first, and he came right at me down the lane. I blocked his shot. I had done it before, and I would do it again. But on this day, at that moment, I became Michael's motivation for the rest of that practice. Every shot he took, no matter whether we were playing five on five or three or three, he had to shoot over ME. With each shot, he said, "Block that."

One time, in that same practice, he drove down the lane, through the entire defense, then back out to the wing, where I was guarding my guy. He ran right at me, shot the ball over my arms, and said, "Block that."

I did block one or two more that day, but he got off more shots than I blocked, and he made the point. It was "Shoot over Bill" day. I was his motivation, and it inspired me that day to work my butt off. We both ended up working harder, simply because he got upset that I blocked that first shot.

Reading Reviews

Most athletes and coaches will tell you they don't read the newspapers or listen to sports radio, but they do. Everyone on the team knows what the beat writers or sports radio voices are reporting. They are talking and writing about us, after all. It's human nature to want to know what they are saying.

Michael used newspaper articles for motivation, but he didn't so much focus on writers or broadcasters, because they were not significant to his progress or success.

Michael liked to read not only what was being written about him in Chicago, but also what was being written or said about him in the cities we visited as well. If we played in Miami, say, and somebody on the team scored 30 or 40 points on him, and then said anything, and I mean anything, about it in the newspaper the next day, Michael used that as his motivation for the next time we played them. We called him "Black Cat," and that cat would not forget. He didn't need to write it down; his

Michael Jordan had high expectations of his teammates and himself, but kids love him. (Photo courtesy of Bill Wennington)

memory about what he perceived as disrespect or a personal slight was like a steel vault. He had a mental logbook he kept, and nothing got erased. The way it worked was, if you scored 30 on him, he would score 40 on you the next time we played. If you scored 40, he would score 50.

You Could Look it Up

He used every little motivation to make himself better. It didn't matter to anyone that I blocked his shot in practice that one day. Big deal, one shot, one lucky jump. But for him, on that day, it was a big deal, and he made it into a huge deal.

That's what I respect most about Michael. He wasn't just happy to be MVP of the league, he had to be the MVP and a champion. He had to be the MVP on the best team. He made the team better, which made him more successful. He was hard on himself, and hard on everybody on the team, so we all understood what our roles were in relation to what Michael was trying to accomplish. With Michael, if you were not ready to play, you were out of there, and he didn't mean off the court, he meant off the team.

Jumping On

The first full year Michael came back, the 1995-96 season, he walked over to me and Steve Kerr and Jud Buechler with a smile on his face at one of our first practices. We had played with him in the spring of the previous season, but we hadn't really gotten to know him yet.

"You guys, you jump on the cape and hold on tight, because I am going to try to buck you off," Michael told us.

He meant it. That's what made it work. He made the 12th guy on the team work as hard as he worked, even if it was just to play one to three minutes a game every other game.

CHAPTER TWO

Scottie Pippen

Scottie Pippen is my favorite Bull. It's not the most popular thing to say in Chicago, because Michael is supposed to be everybody's favorite. And I loved Michael as a person and as a teammate. I just appreciated Scottie more.

Scottie is a passionate person, and he was driven like Michael to succeed. He has said things and done things in his professional career, at the spur of the moment, that have gotten him in trouble, but that is the way he does things. But as a teammate, you could not ask for anyone better than Scottie, and that includes Michael.

Michael is the best player in the history of the game, and he makes everybody better. Michael challenges you every day to be better. Michael will test you every day. But Michael will also let you burn in the coach's eyes to see how you handle the situation. Scottie handled his relationships with his teammates differently, and better, in my opinion.

Scottie Pippen was my favorite Bull. (Photo courtesy of Bill Wennington)

In My Defense

I remember one day we were watching game film at the Berto Center after a game the night before. One of our instructions for that game was that we were not supposed to go help Luc Longley defend the low post. He was supposed to handle that by himself. It wasn't just for that game, actually. Phil believed double-teaming the post compromised the wing and got everybody running around trying to fill holes. He believed one man should be able to guard another man by himself.

One time in the game I was on the floor with Luc, and I was up on the wing, out away from the post. According to Phil's instructions, I couldn't go any lower than the foul line extended. I couldn't double-team the post. Scottie and I were in the high post, past the hash mark, past the three-point line, even, and the ball went into the low post, where Luc was defending. Scottie said to me, "Bill, go help." Obviously, that was against what we practiced, but when you are on the floor, and trying to work as a team, you have to support the whole unit, and believe that you will be supported as well. When Scottie says go, I go. I know Scottie had my guy under control. So I went down, and I double-teamed the low post, and the center threw the ball out, meaning the double-team accomplished its goal.

The next day, watching film, I knew as I was watching it that I had done something that was against what Phil wanted us to do. And Phil was really on my butt.

"Bill, what are you doing? We are not doubling in that situation." To defend myself, I said, "I just thought I should ..." and just as I said "should" Scottie spoke up.

"Phil, I told him to go. I had his guy covered. I wanted him to go down and help."

At that point, I became the biggest Scottie Pippen fan, right there and then. And that sort of thing didn't happen just once. It happened several times, and not just with me, but with all the players on the team. Scottie wasn't exactly covering for us, he was explaining to Phil how things sometimes happen on the floor that don't go according to his plan. He had taken the role of a leader on the floor, and he was defending his decisions to Phil in our film meeting. He was accepting responsibility for the leadership he displayed.

If the same thing happened with Michael, he would let you burn under the coach's examination and grilling and see what you would say in your own defense. Of course, I would never say, "Michael told me to go." I would take the heat, because I was accountable for what I did, no matter the reason. For Michael, it was a test of our willingness to stand up for ourselves. Did Michael respect me more or less because I said it was my decision to go? Who knows? But Scottie didn't test us the same way.

I Wonder?

What was weird about life with the Bulls was that when something like that happened, you got to wondering, "Was that entire incident orchestrated? Did Scottie and Michael and Phil have this all arranged before the game, with Scottie giving us in-game instructions that went against our coach's wishes, then Phil created a scene in film study, and Michael reacted one way to the incident (bad cop) while Scottie reacted another way (good cop), just to see what would happen? Were they trying to find out what kind of character I had?"

With Phil Jackson, master motivator and intellectual basketball coach, such things were possible. You thought that way because it was just so different from what happened on other teams. And it ended up happening to every player on the team. Everyone was tested in much the same way. It made you wonder whether it was all part of a master plan.

Phil was not beyond that kind of psychological ploy.

When I first got to the Bulls, Scottie Pippen was the center of attention. (Photo courtesy of Bill Wennington)

Scottie Was the Man

My first year with the Bulls was the 1993-94 season, the first one Michael did not play because of his initial retirement. In that season, I saw Scottie as No. 1, the top dog, the best player on the team. Scottie turned out to be a better No. 1 than any other No. 1 I ever played with, other than Michael. I know he never took a team to a championship without Michael, but I played with a lot of players—Chris Webber, Mark Aguirre, Sam Perkins—who were supposed to take us to championships, and they did not do it. Scottie was head and shoulders above all of those players in terms of leadership and what he stood for as a team basketball player.

Maybe he learned some of that from watching Michael all those years. But you still had to have some of that kind of drive and desire and leadership qualities within you to make it work the way Scottie did.

Perhaps Scottie Pippen was not the guy to take that last-second shot to win a game 50 percent of the time. Maybe he didn't have the talent by himself to carry a team to a championship. But you remember when Michael had the commercial where he said he missed more shots than he made? That's the truth of it. The same was true for Scottie. He missed, too. But what Scottie represented to me is a player whom I would pick first for my team every time. Even if Michael was available, I would pick Scottie Pippen.

The 1993-94 Bulls

Think about the team Scottie Pippen led in 1993-94, and the atmosphere we were playing in. We had six brand-new guys, guys who were nothing but role players, including me, Steve Kerr, Jud Buechler, Jason Caffey, Randy Brown, and Toni Kukoc, who was like a fish out of water. The guys we had from the championship teams weren't the scoring leaders. They were Horace Grant, Bill Cartwright, B.J. Armstrong, Scott Williams and Will Perdue. We were trying to maintain a success rate the city had become accustomed to, and we were without the No. 1 reason we had that success. It was a hard season to play because of the weight of expectation.

But Scottie Pippen led that team to 55 wins, and only one bad call in a playoff game in New York kept us from going to the NBA finals. He did it without Michael, going further without Michael than Michael ever did without Scottie. Maybe it's apples and oranges, but that season was an indication of what Scottie was capable of doing as a team leader.

CHAPTER THREE

Phil Jackson

Unique

I certainly never had another coach anything like Phil Jackson. I knew of him from his playing days with the New York Knicks, and it was a big deal in New York when he became coach of the Bulls in 1989.

By the time I got to the Bulls, Phil was already declared a genius for pulling three championships out of the Bulls from 1991 through 1993. By 1995, Phil was very deep into his philosophies that extended beyond basketball. He had already written a book from his playing days, entitled *Maverick*, and he had another book out on his coaching experience.

Phil Jackson had a lot of weird philosophies, but I understood a lot of what he was saying. Native Americans view much of life as battle, and in today's world, sports are our battleground. Indian tribes used to fight against other tribes. If you look at the teams in the NBA as tribes, and you look at it as if today our tribe plays the Boston tribe or the Cleveland tribe, and yesterday we played against the Indiana tribe, it creates an entirely different viewpoint that helped us get through the drudgery of a long NBA season.

Phil brought in all that Native American, Indian artifacts, which was fine. He had Native American paraphernalia in his office, and he talked about how we were a tribe. He was trying to create a sense of camaraderie and a willingness to fight for each other.

But the team he was talking to in 1996 wasn't an American audience. He was talking to African Americans, a Croatian, an Australian, a Canadian, and Dennis Rodman. He brought in all this stuff, and initially, none of knew what he was talking about.

He talked about war, and the reasons for war. He talked about the pride of the tribe. He taught us breathing techniques, relaxing modes.

His tribe talk never was us against them. It wasn't a black and white way of looking at our situation. He was telling us "This is what we are. We are a tribe. We are the only ones who know who we are, so we will listen only to each other."

Even now, I'm not sure I understand everything he was trying to tell us.

Yoga Bull

Then there was yoga.

After working us through a strenuous practice, Phil called us together and introduced us to a yoga instructor.

Phil Jackson had a unique way of doing things, but it led to unparalleled success. (AP/WWP)

He was going to help us become one with ourselves. It didn't go over well with anyone. But we all did it.

He had us doing the Lying Dog, the Scrunching Cat, the Tree Standing, but the whole time we were on our knees, and I can't tell you how sore your knees are playing basketball. We were all veterans, and we were all icing our knees after practices and after games, and here Phil had us on our knees trying to get us to relax and achieve oneness with ourselves or something. All we could think about was how nice it was going to feel to put those ice bags on your knees so you could put out the fire. We were putting all of our weight on our knees, and it was unbelievable. But Phil got us all to do it. He convinced Michael and Scottie it was necessary, and so the entire team did it. Granted, every one of us was cussing about having to do this stuff, but not one guy ever left.

Talking to Phil

Some people will tell you that Phil is a bit standoffish. He's got that air of intellectualism that might make him seem unapproachable. But he was never that way with me. To this day, I am able to go up to him and talk with him. He is very accommodating with his time.

When I started doing TV work, he was one of the first sit-down interviews I had to do. He may have been the real first one. Fox asked me to do it, and Phil told the network that he would only do it because it was me doing the interview. He made me feel comfortable in that moment, and the interview went terrifically. I think he is very accommodating to people he knows.

Tex Winter

Tex Winter was one of our assistant coaches, and one of the most knowledgeable basketball men in the world. He was unlike any other basketball man I had ever met. At times it seemed basketball was his entire life.

He knew everything there was to know about basketball, and he tried to tell it all to us. He was always drawing up plays, different actions to run out of the triangle offense he had created.

He was fun to be around, and he was great to use as a resource. But you could never please him with your performance. He was the guy who was never completely happy with what we had done, even when we were winning world championships.

There was always something we could do better. That may be why we played so well. Through it all, including the 72-win season, Tex kept us aware that we could improve.

He was the classic Xs and Os guy. He was always looking for ways to make his triangle offense work more efficiently, and he had created the plan some 50 years earlier. He had a drawing board clipboard with him at all times, and during timeouts he would show us ideas he had drawn up during the game.

Old School

The term "old school" probably was invented with Tex in mind. He was the "work hard, do your job, this is what we are doing, and this is how we are going to do it"

Phil Jackson and Tex Winter watching the in-flight movie, Game Film. (Photo courtesy of Bill Wennington)

kind of guy. He was always in Phil's ear, telling him who was working hard and who was trying to take the day off. He wanted guys off the floor in practice or in games when he saw that the effort wasn't there. Tex wasn't the disciplinarian, but he was the guy telling Phil which of us needed to be disciplined.

For a while, our coaching staff included both Tex and Johnny Bach, and both of them are old school in terms of discipline and work ethic. They are still coaching (Bach has been with the Bulls the last couple of seasons), and I can't believe they can stomach the work ethic attitude of most of today's athletes.

There were occasions when Tex would compliment us, but those compliments came far apart. If you got a compliment from Tex, you remembered it. You probably should write it down and put the date on it, because it was going to be a long time before it happened again.

You had to be a thinking basketball player to completely understand Tex. All he had to do with the Bulls was sell his information to Michael. When Michael bought into what Tex said, everybody else fell in line. Michael had more power than the coaches, but he got along with Tex and understood what he was saying and how it all would benefit him. Tex and Phil sold Michael on the triangle offense, and it paid off handsomely. It's a shame Tex couldn't receive royalties for every time the words "triangle offense" were uttered in describing our success as a team.

Tex was the hardest guy to approach about basketball. You just never knew what he was going to say, although you were pretty sure it wouldn't be full of praise. You sure couldn't ask him about your own game, or why a play didn't work, because he would say, "You need to work harder." The other coaches had more polish, and wouldn't make you feel like such a big loser. Tex was just from the coaching school of thought that praise was for sissies.

Saving Up

It was always fun to watch Tex walk around a hotel, or at a stadium. He was a wanderer. Because he was much older than the other coaches, he didn't have a lot in common with them, and he spent much of his time alone.

I said he was old school as a coach, but that wasn't just in a basketball sense. He was a child of the depression, I guess, and he believed that nothing should be wasted.

So he was frugal. Everything loose, anything that might have some value, that someone else would throw away, he would take.

He was really into shoeboxes. Guys would get a new pair of shoes and throw the box away, and Tex would take the box home to store things. He would tell you, "It's a perfectly good box. Throwing it away is a waste."

He was the same way with food. Not that he picked food out of garbage cans, but he took advantage of free food.

Jim and Jimmy and Frank

Jim Cleamons was the assistant coach you could go to to air your grievances. When Jim left, that role fell to Frank Hamblen. They were both easy to talk to and very approachable. Phil was approachable too, but he liked to maintain his distance, maintain a sense of mystique about him. So the minor stuff, you went to Jim and Frank to discuss.

Jim seemed to have "head coach" written all over him, but he tried it without success in Dallas. Then he took the job coaching a Chicago women's team in something called the American Basketball League. But that didn't stick around long. He rejoined Phil in Los Angeles and picked up a few more championships.

Jimmy Rodgers was our other assistant coach. He had been with championship teams in Boston, and he understood what we were up against on a daily basis. He knew the most about the league, and knew the opposing players as well as anybody on the team.

Chip Schaefer kept our worn-out bodies game ready. (Photo courtesy of Bill Wennington)

Chip Schaefer

Chip Schaefer was our trainer, the one who traveled with us and took care of all of our various aches and pains on a daily basis. He knew his stuff. He was smart, intellectual, well read, and down to earth. He didn't baby us, but he also did a nice job of listening to us when we had an injury concern. He took his job seriously, and since we were his job, we appreciated that.

Chip was an extension of Phil. He was Phil's pipeline for finding out the pulse of the team. He wasn't a stoolie; he was just someone we talked to about our bodies, about how tired we were, about whether we were right physically or wrong physically. Phil knew Chip had that information, and he accessed it when he needed to.

But Chip did a wonderful job maintaining our bodies once we got injured, and he was able to be honest with Phil about when we would be available for practice and games. Phil respected Chip's opinion and acted accordingly.

It is not coincidental that when Phil took the Los Angeles Lakers job, he found a position for Chip Schaefer.

CHAPTER FOUR

Dennis Rodman

To this day, there are people who cannot believe Dennis Rodman became a member of the Chicago Bulls. It would not have happened if Phil Jackson had not signed off on the very controversial idea in the summer of 1995.

Phil had to agree to take Dennis Rodman onto the team. It had to force him to examine all the scenarios, the positives and the negatives. Dennis Rodman came with baggage, and Phil had to ask himself whether carrying the baggage was worth the value Dennis could add to the team.

With the way he played and lived his life, Dennis was obviously a huge distraction. But once Phil realized he was going to get Dennis, he decided to use Dennis's lifestyle as a positive, or at least make positive use out of it. With Dennis on the team, the media was always concentrating on Dennis Rodman and what he was up to the night before rather than asking us, "So, you have a game against

Boston tomorrow night. What are their strengths and how are you going to beat them?"

Instead, the media was talking about how Dennis went out the night before and was seen at the Shelter with Madonna at three in the morning, and what are you going to do about that? The pressure for Michael, for Scottie, for any teammate, was off. It didn't matter how I was going to defend any opponent in the post, it was whether Dennis was going to be awake in time for the game. That was a huge part of the 72-10 year. He took all the pressure off the rest of us. Pressure didn't affect him; he didn't even recognize it much.

There had been talk about who we were going to get to play power forward for the rebuilt Chicago Bulls. The year before we had trouble with rebounding. Horace Grant, a member of the first three-peat teams, had left, and we didn't have anyone to rebound for us.

A lot of talk centered around Jason Williams, the former New Jersey Net. Phil Jackson asked me what I knew about Jason, and I contacted some people I knew who had played with him.

Then the buzz started among the team that they were considering acquiring Dennis Rodman, who had worn out his welcome in the staid community of San Antonio, Texas. We all kind of found out about it at practice one day. Then everyone started telling their own Dennis Rodman stories.

I had been playing in Chicago for two years, and I knew the possibility of adding Dennis Rodman to our roster would be big news. I wasn't a part of the team when it had its big rivalry years with the Pistons, but I knew Dennis was not appreciated in Chicago. Bringing him in was going to be monumental.

Getting to Know Who?

I remember when the news hit that we had traded for Dennis Rodman. Dennis came in the first day of training camp and was in shape. He was on time, and he was on his best behavior.

We were all kind of surprised that Dennis was now a teammate, although he didn't feel like a teammate right away. Nobody knew how to approach him. No one would talk to Dennis, because they didn't know how he was going to react. We were going to let sleeping dogs lie.

At the time, I had the same business agent as Dennis. We had actually spoken about that on the floor during a game one time, when we were on different teams. One day we were in the locker room, in the training room at the Berto Center, our practice facility, and we were all talking about Dennis. Somebody said 'Has anyone talked to Dennis yet?' And it turned out, nobody had. He had been our teammate for some time, and none of us had gone to the trouble of welcoming him and making small talk. Had it been anybody else, such pleasantries would have been automatic.

I was surprised to find out that Dennis had been snubbed in that way, although I hadn't bothered to talk to him yet, either.

"You guys haven't talked to him yet?" I said.

So I was elected to be the guy who would try to communicate with Dennis Rodman. They knew I would talk to anybody, I guess.

I thought, "Sure, leave it to the Canadian guy to break the ice with the crazy guy."

So I did. I said hi, and reminded him that we had the same agent. I knew he was into motorcycles, because he had gotten injured in a motorcycle accident when he was with the San Antonio Spurs. So I told him I was getting a motorcycle built for myself. We talked about that for a while. He didn't say much. But I told him, "I'm glad you are here with the Bulls. I think we have a chance to do some great things now that you are here." And he said thanks.

I went back and told the other guys it was O.K. Dennis was approachable. I'm not sure they all bought it. It took a long time for everybody to have an understanding of where Dennis was coming from.

Dennis Distraction

Things were going really well in that 1995-96 season. We were breaking records the whole season, fastest team to 20 wins, fastest team to 30 wins. But it wasn't until after the all-star break that people started saying, "Maybe these guys can win 70 games." It wasn't until we got to 60 or 65 wins that the media was coming into the locker room saying, "Is it going to happen?"

What kept the media at bay? We had Dennis, and the media was so focused on the everyday goings on in Dennis's life that it forget to concentrate on the remarkable level of basketball we were playing.

Then we got into March, and all of a sudden people started to tell us, "You guys are really good." It was if Dennis Rodman had made everyone fail to notice our record.

Dennis Good

I have said that Scottie Pippen is the first player I would want on my personal basketball team. The second player I would select is Dennis Rodman. In fact, I think that would be a great three-on-three team. I could shoot the ball as much as I wanted, Dennis would get the rebound, and Scottie would pass the ball back to me.

For all of his odd behavior, Dennis had a lot in common with Michael. He would do whatever it took to win a basketball game. He knows the game as well or better than anybody else in the league.

What he does off the court is another matter. What he did off the court was for publicity and money. He is a smart man, but he is an individual. And in a basketball sense, when it comes down to it, if there is a ball rolling off the floor, and everybody started 50 feet from the ball, against anybody in the world, Dennis Rodman would get the basketball.

Even though he wasn't the friendliest guy around, he did a tremendous job learning about his teammates. He knew what his teammates liked to do with the ball, and he knew how everybody shot the basketball. He knows the opposition players as well, knows what their shots do off the rim, knows what they do when they get tired.

I was privileged to have Dennis as a teammate those three seasons. He respects and loves the game more than he loves himself.

Dennis Deep

There were obviously a great number of late nights, and with Dennis around, the stories that came out of those nights were sometimes of epic proportion. But Dennis has already told most of those stories, or made them up, or covered them up to protect the innocent.

I remember one night in Coconut Grove, Florida, that started as just another party night, but ended up being very revealing in terms of how I thought of Dennis Rodman.

When we played in Miami, we stayed at a very unique hotel in the hot party area of Coconut Grove. Across the street from our hotel was a small mall, and in the mall was a sports bar named for former Miami Dolphins quarterback Dan Marino.

It was midnight. I was in a VIP room in the back. It had a big plate glass window where you could see out into the bar, but patrons couldn't see in. We were back there because we were the Bulls, the basketball equivalent of the Beatles, and Dennis needed some privacy.

I was in there with some other players, our longtime broadcaster, Johnny "Red" Kerr, and one newspaper reporter. Back in those days, players and the media co-mingled, and there was an unspoken rule about what was on the record and what wasn't. In this case, it was an off-the-record moment, but the reporter was pushing the envelope, digging in at Dennis to get a story out of him.

The story he got was that Dennis Rodman knows basketball.

Dennis told him that he watched a lot of tape, especially of shooters. He noticed when they are fresh and just in the game, their arms are in a certain position, and their motion and follow through are complete. But after 15 minutes, their arms get tired and their hand doesn't follow through as much and they miss the shot short. But some players push their arms more when they get tired, and their shot is going to go long. Dennis knew that kind of stuff. He broke down a lot of players in the league that night, and I actually learned a lot about rebounding. From Dennis Rodman, in a bar.

I learned a lot about Dennis that night, about how he approaches the game of basketball. I don't think anyone realizes the amount of thought that went into his game.

The unfortunate part of that night was that ended at about 3:30 in the morning. I made it back to my room, but Dennis stayed after. We flew to Detroit the next day, and had a practice in the late morning. Dennis was there, but I don't know how he did it.

How Did This Happen?

You have to wonder, in the history of professional sports, was there ever a more unusual player transaction than Dennis Rodman ending up with the Bulls? I didn't join the Bulls until after Dennis had left the Detroit Pistons, but I knew that the organization hated the old Bad Boys, and as a result hated Dennis. He had put a scar on Scottie Pippen's face, and had been such a nemesis that the idea of him being on the Bulls was very, very hard for a lot of people to appreciate.

Once Dennis got there, and he and Michael had a meeting of the minds, it became apparent that Dennis was one of those special athletes who creates a unique attitude from other players. You hate to play against him, but when he is on your team, you love him. He works hard, and whatever he needs to do to win, he will do.

He was a theatrical player. He was a showman, and he overemphasized diving for loose balls. He found out there was a way to be marketed with that kind of behavior. Sure, it got him in trouble at times. But when he played for the Bulls, he was the best basketball player he could be. He did all the things he needed to do to make the team better.

Motorcycle Maintenance

Phil Jackson was into motorcycles, and I had gotten to the point where I was having a motorcycle built especially for me. Luc Longley was having one built for himself as well. When Dennis came, we all knew he rode, because he had been in an accident in San Antonio where he hurt himself, just before the playoffs.

Phil was sort of nondecisive about whether guys could ride or not. He rode himself, so he didn't feel he could tell us not to ride. He never said no, he never said yes.

Dennis had a security guard named George who helped me learn how to ride. I became accomplished enough that I went up to Dennis one day and told him if he ever needed someone to ride with to call me up.

One day, sure enough, Dennis called me at home and said, "Do you want to ride?"

I went over to his house, and we rode to downtown Chicago. We didn't go far, just to find a place to go to have lunch, ride around the city and head back to the north shore.

It was an amazing experience.

I wear a helmet when I ride, and I wear a shirt that covers my whole body. Dennis wore a tank top, no helmet, maybe a bandana over his head. He had his tattoos on display, and earrings, jewelry sparkling in the sunlight.

Every single car that passed us that first day slowed up, and it was unreal how many people were riding around with cameras. There must have been hundreds of photos of Dennis taken that day on the highway. We were doing 45, 55 miles an hour, and drivers were in their cars trying to get closer to us to get a good shot. They were almost driving me off the road to get closer to him.

It got to the point that, when Dennis and I would ride, George would drive in a car behind us to keep people off of us and allow us to enjoy our ride.

CHAPTER FIVE

Toni Kukoc

The championship teams from 1996 through 1998 had the best threesome of players ever assembled in Michael Jordan, Scottie Pippen and Dennis Rodman. But the unsung hero of the group might have been Toni Kukoc.

Toni was from the European country of Croatia, and he had come over to the Bulls after a successful professional playing career in Italy. He was going to be the best European player ever to come to the United States. Jerry Krause, the Bulls' general manager, was putting a huge campaign effort into getting him to come over, and he was upsetting Scottie Pippen in the process, because Scottie was waiting for a new contract. The Bulls would not do anything for Scottie until they had Toni in the fold.

When Toni came to the United States, it was a very difficult adjustment for him for a lot of reasons.

I had a little history with Toni. He and I played against each other before we got together in Chicago. I played against Toni in Italy. In fact, we played against each other for the Italian Championship the spring before I came to the Bulls. I was on Knorr Bologna and he was on Benetton Treviso. My team won the championship series in five games.

Toni came to the Bulls and got a lot of money and I came to the Bulls and didn't, so I guess that Italian championship didn't matter as much as individual talent.

Drink Down

In Europe, things are different. When I played over there, we used to have team meals all the time, and there would be two bottles of wine on the table and you could have a glass of wine with your dinner, with the team, even before a game.

When we were with the Bulls, we were on our first west coast road trip in the fall of 1993, and I ran into Toni sitting alone at a restaurant in Seattle. He was having lunch by himself because, in the NBA, unless you make arrangements at practice to go out for a meal with a teammate, or you have a regular eating partner or two, you end up eating by yourself. Toni was still getting accustomed to everyone on the team, and hadn't developed any great friendship that would allow him to have a regular lunchtime partner.

He was also having trouble finding his role on the basketball floor, which may have added to his difficulty in making friends.

So he was out by himself having lunch in this restaurant, and it was the day of a game against the SuperSonics.

I walked up to his table and asked him, "Are you playing tonight?" He said, "Yeah, why do you ask?"

"You're drinking a beer," I said.

"This is what I do before a game," he said. "I have a beer or a glass of wine before a game."

I had to tell him things are a little different over here.

"I don't object to having a beer, one beer, with lunch seven hours before we play a game, but if a passerby sees you having a beer right now, and you don't have a good game tonight, what do you think they are going to talk about?"

Toni is obviously very European, and I told him I agreed with him, that it wasn't going to do any harm, but I told him it was not good for him to do that here.

Toni Cried

The day before Michael officially retired in the fall of 1993, everybody on the team kind of knew it was going to happen, except for Toni. He wasn't in the inner circle yet, and he just didn't know. I remember Steve Kerr and I were talking in the dressing room, wondering what we had gotten ourselves into, because we had signed to play with a championship team and Michael Jordan.

Suddenly, we were on an ordinary team.

Toni heard us talking, and he was really distraught. He began questioning himself, because he had really waited for the right moment to come to the NBA. He was a superstar in Europe, and he had no reason to come to the United States, except for the chance to play with Michael. The Bulls had drafted him way back in 1990. He had held

It took some time, but Toni Kukoc began to fit in with the guys. (Photo courtesy of Bill Wennington)

off for three years, waiting for the right moment, and when the right moment came, suddenly it was pulled out from under him. Michael wasn't going to play, and Toni wasn't going to get to play with him.

Toni was the most upset member of the team. The rest of us understood it was a business. But Toni saw it as a missed opportunity for him and it wasn't going to work out the way he hoped it would work out.

In hindsight, I think it worked out better for Toni. It gave him more of a learning curve, more of a process, to be more a part of the team. Without Michael around, there was more of the load put on him in the basketball games. If Michael had been there from the start, it would have been easier for Phil to hold Toni out even more. Phil was hard on him anyway, and so was Scottie because Toni was considered a Jerry Krause pet. When Michael came back, Michael was tremendously hard on Toni. But that first year, without Michael, was a good experience for Toni because it forced him to be more a part of the offensive game plan, and he had responsibilities to the team.

Toni Laughed

Toni was a fun guy to be around, when he was having fun. Coming to the United States, he had to break some of his old habits from Italy. In Italy, you could yell at your teammates, especially the young ones. You could be a real tyrant about it, and once he got here, he was very aggressive, telling everyone what to do. We had to get Toni to understand a little bit that he had to present his ideas in another way, or everyone would be very upset at him.

But he was different in other ways, and maybe it was all part of being European. If we would do something as a group, like say we would go to a movie, and he didn't like the movie, he would just walk out without saying anything. If he was with one person or with 13 people, he would just leave. That took some getting used to.

I remember when the Austin Powers movie first came out, Toni was always whistling that song from the movie, the "Bossa Nova." It was never ending, the same tune over and over, and it got to where people would start whistling it without knowing they were doing it, and then everybody else would scream for that guy to shut up. Toni started that, and he would laugh, because he knew he had planted the seed.

Toni Kukoc had game. (AP/WWP)

The Waiter

It was fun playing with Toni because he could really pass the ball, and he liked passing. For a 6-10, 6-11 guy, to be able to pass the ball the way he did, was unbelievable. Jerry Krause said he was known as The Waiter, because he served the ball so well to his teammates.

Phil Jackson really took a lot out on him. I don't know about the Phil Jackson-Jerry Krause relationship, but Toni Kukoc was Jerry's big find, a very big public coup in Jerry's eyes, and Jerry had compared him to Michael, calling him the European Michael Jordan or something like that. Honestly, a lot of that first training camp in 1993 was spent just in awe just of how much abuse Toni was taking. It was really difficult for Toni. He took a lot, from a variety of sources. Scottie was on him a little bit because Toni had played against the Dream Team in the Olympics, and Phil was hard on him because he was Jerry's guy. Somehow, through it all, Toni learned how to play in the NBA.

That first year, all of Toni's work and abuse came down to the 1.8 seconds, when Scottie Pippen refused to go into the playoff game against the New York Knicks because Phil Jackson had drawn up the play for Toni to take the last shot. Toni gained a lot of respect from teammates and the NBA because he made the shot and won the game. As upset as Scottie was at the time, I think he knew Toni bailed him out big time. He proved himself to be a guy who could make that shot.

Phil did realize what he had in Toni, even as he put him through all those difficult paces. For Phil to call that last second play for Toni against New York in a big game for us, it was a sign he had the confidence in Toni to make

it. That was the defining moment for him and his basketball career with the Bulls.

After that, Toni became a guy we could ride. We all
have moments in our game, at the NBA level, when it
becomes clear to the public and to the coaches that we can
play the game with a certain effectiveness. That was a huge
step for Toni, to make that shot.

That shot helped bind Scottie and Toni a little bit,
even if it seemed to pit them against each other. Scottie
respects talent and respects the game. If you could play and
knew the game, there was a respect that came out of that,
and it grew. I think they became friends on a basketball
level. That doesn't mean they watched TV together. We
didn't have a lot of that. Steve and Jud and Luc did that
some, but we weren't the kind of team to hang out together when we were home. We all had families to go home to.

Toni Can Play

Toni was a starter who came off the bench. He could
have started with any team in the NBA, but because of the
makeup of the team we had, he had to play off the bench.

He fit in really well and provided offense for the
bench when things weren't working out for someone in the
starting lineup. He was 6-11, but he could replace anyone
on the floor. He could bring up the ball, he could play the
two spot, the three, the four, or the five spot if teams went
small on us.

We had four guys on the team who could play just
about anywhere on the floor.

No matter who was having a bad game or was in foul trouble, we could go to Toni. You didn't have to bring in a new guy in. He helped everybody become a better player. That's what real stars do.

Once Michael came back, and he discovered how well Toni could play, Michael started giving Toni respect, and that helped Toni develop even more. When Michael came, Toni had already earned the respect of other guys, and Phil had already started to respect Toni. Michael came back to play the last 13 games of the 1995 season, and I think he knew right away that Toni could play at his level and help him get back to the NBA Finals.

CHAPTER SIX

Luc Longley

Let me start this off by saying I'm Canadian, and Luc Longley is Australian. We are both members of the British Commonwealth, so we had a bond.

Our bond was that we were both seven feet tall, we were both not American, playing in an American basketball league, and we were both looking for some respect and recognition in the league. The Commonwealth thing, that wasn't really a factor. It's not like we had a club or meetings or anything.

Luc Longley came to the Bulls in a trade that sent Stacey King to the Minnesota Timberwolves. Luc had built a reputation as a mild-mannered center with some offensive skills and a big body. He had worn out his welcome in Minnesota, and he came to the Bulls not as a savior or a superstar but as a role player, which better fit his skills and his personality. He was a real center, where Stacey was undersized for the position and wasn't developing the way he was expected to in Chicago.

I don't really recall the two of us ever having any sort of personal confrontation, even though we were competing against each other for playing time. We practiced against each other every day, but we were both laid back enough that it never really got ugly. He was the starter, but I was a backup who got a lot of playing time. We were completely different players, which made us valuable to the team in different ways.

Centers of Attention

I remember times when Phil would get mad at me for letting Luc get close post-up position, and I remember Phil getting mad at Luc when I would hit my little 15-foot jump shot. That was my bread and butter, offensively, and Phil would yell, "Luc, what did you THINK he was going to do?" We pushed each other to become better, and I think we both accomplished that over the years we were together.

Luc and I were two different players, that's for sure. I was more of a runner, more athletic. The Bulls tried to get me to be bigger and stronger, and I did increase both my size and my strength over the years. When I got to the Bulls, I was at about 250 pounds, and by the time I left I was up to 280 pounds. They made me bigger, and they wanted me to change my game, to be more like Luc. Where Luc would roll to the basket and try to finish there, I would always step out and take the 15-foot jumper. Through my 13 years, that never changed. I didn't play as much because of it, but I was often successful being who I was.

Luc Longley was the starter, and I understood the decision. (AP/WWP)

The year Luc got hurt and I started for 12 or 14 games in a row, and in those games I started, my stats were better than his as a starter. I know he was worried. Luc thought he had lost his starting job to me. Maybe I was a better scorer, but Luc was bigger, and he defended the post better. I think I understood that, even though I wasn't happy about it.

No Worries

Luc liked to have a good time, and maybe that was part of his problems. He came from a background that was not as fast-paced as the American lifestyle. He didn't always focus on the game at hand. He wasn't intense. He was a happy guy, and he brought us the Australian phrase "No worries," which just sounded so good coming out of his mouth with that Aussie accent he had.

Luc was a people person. We would go to dinner as a group, and Luc had a habit of ordering food for everybody. He would order appetizers for the whole crowd, and then some. By the time we finished the appetizers he ordered, we wouldn't want our entrees because we were already done eating.

He was just a fun kid. He tried to do his best on the basketball floor, but he really just wanted to have fun. He never wanted to hurt anybody. He actually seemed to love everybody he knew on the team.

He drove Michael Jordan crazy.

Three Heads Are Better

Luc and I were two heads of the second three-headed monster.

Through the first three championships, from 1991 through 1993, the Bulls always had three centers to depend on. It was Bill Cartwright, Will Perdue and Stacey King. Between them, they had 18 fouls to offer when the Bulls played against a big, quality center. They weren't called upon to score much. They just had to play defense and make sure the other team's center didn't have a field day inside.

By the time we got around to winning our championships later in the decade, we knew how the three-headed monster thing worked. In 1995-96, it was me, Luc and James Edwards, the former Piston. In 1996-97, it was me, Luc and Robert Parish, the former Celtic. In 1997-98, it was me, Luc and Joe Kleine, who had been around the league for years. In our incarnation, the third center wasn't used as much as he was in the early 1990s.

We understood for the team to be successful, we had to play our roles in the middle. Everybody knew the key components of our success on offense. Michael was the No. 1 guy, Scottie and Toni were the next two guys, Ron Harper could still score and was a good defender. Dennis played great defense and got 14 rebounds a night. We had all the positions covered by superstar talent except at the "5," which was the center. That job fell to the three-headed monster.

Luc was the starter for our championship teams because he was a very good ball-handler, and in the triangle offense the ball had to go through the post, and then back out in most cases. Luc also was bigger than me, with his big, wide body. When he put his mind to it, he could be aggressive on defense, and he had some good offensive moves.

We had some large loads to play against in those years, like Shaquille O'Neal of Orlando, Rik Smits at Indiana, Patrick Ewing in New York, and Hakeem Olajuwon in Houston. We needed a big body inside just to slow things down.

Crashing the Wave

Luc's most significant injury came in November of 1996. It was certainly a unique mishap, and I remember just how much tension existed because of it. But it makes for a great story.

We were in Los Angeles, preparing to play the Clippers during our usual November west coast trip, and we had an extra day off for California fun and games. Jud Buechler, our surfin' dude teammate, took Luc out body-surfing, which was an activity Longley had participated in as a kid growing up in Australia. Jud, of course, knew the best places to go in Los Angeles for bodysurfing.

(The only reason I wasn't there was because I had rented a motorcycle and went riding. I wonder what might have happened if I had gone.)

At some point in the day, Luc got picked up by a wave, and it dropped him hard on a sandbar. As I remember it, he was going forward, and he hit the sand with his shoulder. That happens a lot in bodysurfing, where a wave picks you up and then suddenly it just stops. You are three feet in the air, you have this momentum built up, and then you are dropped.

Hitting that sandbar with his shoulder hurt him a lot, but the pain was only part of Luc's problem. He was panicked, because he didn't know how Phil was going to react to the news. An injury playing basketball is one thing, an injury bodysurfing, for a seven-foot starting center, was an entirely different matter.

Luc and Jud got back to the hotel, and Jud ran into me and Steve and told us what happened. Luc was unsure what to do. He knew he had to call the trainer, Chip Schaefer, and he knew he needed a doctor. But he really, really didn't want to make that call.

When I saw Jud, he thought he was going to get in trouble because he was with Luc, and had pretty much put him in the position to get hurt. Jud wasn't playing a lot, and he was worried his playing time would disappear completely, or that he might even get cut.

When I saw Luc, I was amazed at how scared he was. Although his position was secure with the team, he also thought he was going to get cut from the team, or his contract was going to get ripped up, because he had been doing something they didn't really allow players to do.

It's not like his contract had a clause in that disallowed surfing, but it certainly didn't say surfing was allowed. Jud and Luc sat in the hotel, terrified of telling Phil and Jerry Krause.

When Luc got around to telling Phil, I don't think Phil was mad that Luc had been bodysurfing. He was just mad Luc had gotten hurt bodysurfing. Luc went on the injured list and was there for about four to six weeks, and everything worked out all right.

Luc had to wear a huge shoulder pad for weeks, and he looked like the Hunchback of Notre Dame. That Disney movie had come out about that time, and so we all gave Luc Hunchback toys and dolls. Luc took a lot of abuse over that.

CHAPTER SEVEN

The Rest of the Lineup

In my seven years in the NBA before joining the Bulls, I had been on good teams. I was with the Dallas Mavericks in 1988 when we went to conference finals against the Los Angeles Lakers and took them to seven games. We had Mark Aguirre, Rolando Blackman, Derek Harper, Detlef Schrempf, Sam Perkins, Roy Tarpley, and James Donaldson. We had a good team, but we didn't work together as a team. We didn't respect each other as a team enough to win. We didn't all do our jobs to our fullest. We may have worked hard, but we didn't do what it takes to win a basketball game. I didn't know that until I joined the Bulls and saw how it can be different, and better.

You don't think Randy Brown wanted to shoot more and play more for the Bulls? He did. But he was there to bring the ball up the floor and to play defense as a backup to Ron Harper.

You don't think I wanted to start over Luc Longley? I wanted to play 30 minutes a game, but my job was to come off the bench, provide energy, pound the life out of whatever center was out there, and hit a couple of shots.

Steve Kerr was supposed to come off the bench, spot up in three-point range, and get the kickoff from Michael and Scottie as they were driving to the basket.

Jud Buechler was supposed to be fundamentally sound, play great defense and take a couple shots, again in support of the starters.

Toni Kukoc was supposed to be the scorer off the bench. That was his job.

Star Bright, Star Light

When Ron Harper came into the league out of Miami of Ohio, he was a great scorer. He played in that capacity with the Cleveland Cavaliers and the Los Angeles Clippers for years. He was never Michael Jordan, but he was the next best thing.

But Ron had an injury along the way that affected his offensive ability. So when he came to the Bulls, Ron had to change his mentality from being a scorer to being a role player. When you think about Ron Harper's time with the Cavaliers, you know that he was a hot commodity. When he came to us, he had to take a step back personally for the benefit of the team. Nobody really knew whether he could do that. That was a big step back for Ron. He had to decide, "I am going to sacrifice my game." But that is part of the team aspect that isn't completely understood. It's kind of like marriage. There are compromises and sacrifices made for the greater good.

Movie Night

One of the funniest things of the 72-10 year occurred in Salt Lake City, Utah. We spent almost every Thanksgiving on the road, because the circus was booked for the United Center over that period. I know in my time with the Bulls we spent Thanksgiving in Dallas, Salt Lake City, and Vancouver.

One year we ended up in Salt Lake City for the holiday, and we all decided we were going to go to the movies on Thanksgiving evening. It was a large group—Jud, Steve, Randy, me, Luc, Dickey Simpkins, and I don't remember if anybody else came.

We were walking to the movies, because the theater was about three blocks from our hotel, and we ran into Michael, who was also going to the movies. He had his security guards, about five of them, and they were all going to the same movie we were going to. It being Salt Lake City on Thanksgiving, and I guess the movie was the only viable entertainment option.

We got to the theatre, and the place was absolutely empty. It was before dinner on Thanksgiving, and nobody was out. We had the theatre practically to ourselves. When our showing of the movie was over and we all walked outside, we figured it would be just as quiet as it was when we went in. But the lobby was packed for the 7 o'clock show. People were lined up waiting to get in, out the door and around the corner. It was one of those holiday blockbuster movies, very popular. I wish I could remember which one.

All of a sudden, all of those people saw Michael. There had to be 300 people waiting in line to get in to see this movie, and when they saw Michael, they started following us. It was more important for those people to get

Whether it was the movies or the beach, it was easier to travel incognito without Michael Jordan. (Photo courtesy of Bill Wennington)

an autograph from Michael than to get in to see the movie they had been waiting for. We all became security guards for Michael. But the people didn't care who we were. They didn't see other members of this championship-caliber team. They just saw some big guys who were in their way trying to get to Michael.

Freedom of Speech

Ron Harper stutters. It was something he had to learn to get over, and it was obviously something that was very difficult for him growing up. Through his NBA career, there had been stories written about how he dealt with this personal issue, and then it became clear that he had found a way to handle the problem. By the time he was with the Bulls, it wasn't a debilitating thing for him, and he was accustomed to the problems it presented in personal relationships as well as in his dealings with the media.

But we also used to give him a hard time about it.

Ron stuttered most when he got excited or angry. In those situations, he couldn't focus enough on what he was saying to avoid the stutter. There were guys on the team who loved to get Ron riled up, just to hear him go off.

Ron came into the league as a superstar for Cleveland, but he had a horrible injury that affected his game. He went to the Los Angeles Clippers and played well, but there started to be questions about how much Ron could do. We needed someone to come in and be a point guard in the absence of John Paxson. Ron came to us and excelled, especially when he was teamed up with Michael. The two of them made for a dominant backcourt. Ron was still a great defensive player, and he had enough offensive skills to make the other team stay honest on him, unable to go with the double-team defense on Michael.

Having Michael put Ron back on the right track. From a basketball standpoint, he had the most to overcome. You think about what Dennis had to overcome, and what Michael had to deal with because of what happened to his father. But Ron came in as a player with one kind of attitude, a superior, dominant attitude, and he had to become a different, less dominant player in order to be a big part of what ended up being one of the greatest teams ever.

Ron scored when he needed to score, he really handled the ball well, and he played great defense for us. He bought into the triangle offense in a big way and fed off of what Scottie and Michael represented defensively. He helped us more than what a lot of people give him credit for, in being a catalyst to winning a championship.

A Little Short

Even the best basketball players in the world, the ones with all the hops, miss dunks on occasion. Michael missed them, too. But I remember one dunk Ron missed that was one of the funniest moments we had on the floor.

Ron and Michael were very competitive with each other. They were always talking about their games, about who is stronger, who is better. Remember, when Ron came into the league, he was there to challenge Michael, and he did so in a lot of Bulls-Cleveland games.

Ron Harper had a bit of a rivalry with Michael Jordan. (AP/WWP)

They would talk about, "Remember when I scored 40 on this guy," and the other guy would say, "Yeah, well I scored 45 on him." They were like sibling rivals in that respect.

Before one game at the United Center, they got to talking about their dunking ability. So, once the game got going, we were in the third quarter and Ron got a steal at midcourt. He was all by himself, and I think he was trying to show Michael something, to prove he could come up with an impressive dunk. But on the way up he planted wrong, he didn't get the lift he needed, and he didn't get high enough to make the dunk.

I have never seen Michael laugh that hard. He laughed all the way through the next possession, and then got taken out of the game, sat on the bench and laughed some more, pounding everybody on the back, slapping his knee, the whole bit. Ron just stood out on the floor, glaring at Michael, knowing he would never hear the end of it.

Getting Along

We were a team that just got along. We were extremely different, all of us. There was nothing Steve Kerr had in common with Dennis Rodman. Luc Longley and Michael Jordan were different people. But we got along in a way that now seems nearly impossible.

It was such a cool thing, to walk into a restaurant, see a teammate and know you would be invited to sit down with him. It's not like that anymore. But back then, it didn't matter who you were on the team, you were welcome and wanted. You could be rookie Jason Caffey at the end of the bench, or a Rusty LaRue who never played, but you were welcome wherever your teammate was.

Moth, Meet Flame

Steve Kerr and I were the most media-accessible members of the Bulls team. But we both argued over which one of us went out of our way the most to get in front of the TV cameras and radio microphones.

When Steve came to the Bulls in 1993, he had already started to think about what was going to come for him professionally after basketball. We both understood we wanted to get into broadcasting, because the opportunities are good for someone who can speak well and handle the occasional pressure. We both made ourselves available to the media, in an attempt to learn as much about the business as possible, and to be accommodating to the men and women who followed us everywhere we went.

I was always pretty straightforward with what I was doing, and I enjoy people, so I would just make myself available. If someone had to have a question answered, I would be there. Steve would do it the back-door way. He would wait a little longer until most reporters were gone, then he would do individual interviews with the last guy around. When you watched the news that night, I would be in the mass interviews, and he would be in a singular interview. I caught a lot of heat for that, from him.

But I was the one who had a trophy made for Moth of the Year, going to the player who made a habit of approaching the bright lights. I gave it to Steve first, even though he always talked about giving it back to me because I was more moth than he was. I don't think Steve ever accepted the award. I believe I still have it, somewhere at the Berto Center. Maybe I will mail it to him, now that he is a big TV guy with Turner Broadcasting.

I'm Not John

John Paxson was the quintessential point guard partner to Michael Jordan, and was famous in Chicago for playing with Jordan on the first three championship teams. He hit the shot that won the 1993 final against Phoenix, and is still one of the most respected athletes in Chicago.

Steve Kerr was clearly brought in to play the John Paxson role for the second coming of the championship Bulls. But I don't think Steve ever thought of himself as that. He didn't want to play in John's shadow. Steve believed he would earn his own merit with the team. I remember when he first got to the team that he was asked questions about being the next Paxson, and he wouldn't even talk about it. He didn't have to. He came in with a reputation as a great shooter.

As much fun as he is, he was the most dedicated person I know. To be that great a shooter, you have to be willing to work at it. When he got down and struggling with his shooting, he was a different person. He would get so down on himself, we would have to pull him out of it. He would really beat himself up, more so than anyone I had seen before.

He wanted to make every shot he took. There were times when he was too hard on himself. He put that much pressure on himself to be the best shooter he could be.

Michael and Steve

I remember the time Steve Kerr hit Michael Jordan in the fist with his eye.

Michael had just come back from retirement, and Steve was up and coming, trying to prove himself a worthy teammate. B.J. Armstrong was getting pushed aside a little bit at point guard, or had lost favor with Phil. Michael had an awful lot going on in his life, but he was trying to make his comeback and get things working again on the court. We all know how that turned out.

We were having a physical practice, and Michael was in a particularly ornery mood that day. It became overly physical and Michael gave Steve a kind of a shot that was unwarranted. The next time down the court, Steve gave Michael a shot back. We are not talking punches here, just severe body contact, a little more physical than necessary. Steve was just standing up for himself, something that Michael has always said he respected in opponents and teammates. But Michael wasn't thinking that way at the moment; he said, "That's it," and they squared up.

Michael swung at Steve and hit him, and Steve came back at him. We all separated the two, and then Michael left practice right away. The rest of us finished the work-out, and by the end Michael had come back. He apologized to Steve and apologized to the team. And I know Michael respected Steve more because he stood up for himself.

Steve's Shot

Steve's moment came in the 1997 NBA Finals against Utah. He was not having a great shooting series, as I recall. There was a timeout in the last seconds of the sixth game at the Delta Center in Salt Lake City. We were leading the series 3-2, and we were trying to avoid the seventh game.

We were losing by a point. A play was drawn up, and Steve was an option on the play. Obviously, Michael would get the ball. As they walked onto the court after the time-out, Steve went to Michael and said, "Get me the ball. I will make the shot." So Michael penetrated, drew the double team, and Steve was in position to make your basic 15-footer at the foul line. And of course, Michael got him the ball and Steve hit the shot to win the game.

Steve believed in himself so much, and he knew he could do it. He wanted to let Michael know he could count on him. Steve loved that moment. I remember hearing him say that what had just occurred was every kid's dream, to hit the shot to win a championship. The stars were lined up right, things worked out, and he did what everyone always hopes to do.

Steve Kerr hits the winning shot versus the Jazz in the 1997 Finals. (AP/WWP)

Just Jud

Jud Buechler was the guy we called "Fundy." That stood for Fundamentally Sound. He was a California beach bum, a volleyball player, a basketball player. He loved volleyball and loved to be on the beach. We would always have these conversations about what we would do after basketball, and the classic line I remember from Jud was, "I don't know what I am going to be doing after basketball, but I know where I am going to be doing it. I will be in Del Mar, California, on the beach. Whatever I do, it will be there."

When you look at Jud, you think of all those Beach Boy songs. He was the 1990s version of those guys. He rides the tasty wave, plays some volleyball, and knows all the California lingo. I think Jud and his family are in Del Mar right now.

But, for a surfin' dude, he took his basketball job seriously. He did the little things. He's actually the kind of guy you hardly ever see in the game anymore.

He knew how to make a jump stop and make a perfect pass out of it. He knew how to set the perfect pick and roll right out of it.

He was a very good athlete. He couldn't jump all that well, and he wasn't the fastest guy on the team, but he worked as hard as anybody, and he didn't make mistakes. He was a great guy to have on the team.

Chicago Randy

Randy Brown, the backup point guard, was the team comic. Randy had funny voices and could imitate people really well. He had characters he did, and he was a fast talker. He was really smart, too, but he was so funny that he could always relax a tense situation. He helped a lot of team meetings that way.

Randy also helped everybody relate to everybody else. He was the feel-good guy on the team. He helped everybody understand each other, where we were coming from, who we were. He did a lot of little things to make sure there were no misunderstandings on the team.

It was pretty well known that Randy was the first guy from Chicago to be selected to play for the Bulls. Jerry Krause had this thing about Chicago guys, thinking they would have too many personal pressures in town to be able to play effectively. Well, Randy certainly had personal issues to deal with. He has three brothers, and they all look exactly like Randy, and they were always around. They are all still around today.

Randy was one of those guys everybody liked, everybody had fun with.

He was brought into the team to play defense and bring the ball up. He was one of the guys who wanted to play a lot more than he did. But he was third on the depth chart at his position, behind Ron Harper and Steve Kerr. He was one of those players who had to accept a lot less personal playing time than he thought he was capable of in order to help the team succeed.

Randy had another skill that was just odd. You could ask him about a high school kid from the city of Chicago and he would know him, his mom, his dad, his brother, his sister. But then you would talk about some kid coming out of Ohio, and he would know his entire family, and his coach. Randy knew everyone. He had a talent for making acquaintances. He was one of the first guys in the league who had a cell phone and he used it all the time. If you needed information, he could get on that phone and find it out for you—fast.

A Moment's Reflection

I remember when Jason Caffey came in as a rookie in 1995. He joined us for the 72-10 season, so he was seeing the best the world of pro basketball had to offer.

After practice one day, just before the all-star break, he was looking around the locker room, slowly examining the players he was with and the situation he was in.

He said to me, "This is unbelievable. Is it always like this?"

I said, "Jason, it is never like this. You need to take notes and see everything that happens this year, because it will never be like this again."

CHAPTER EIGHT

Hanging Around

We were the Bulls, the most adored team in all of basketball, in all of sports. By the time we had won the first championship of the second three-peat, in 1996, we were surrounded by the rich and the famous.

The games in New York were always huge media events, because we had a rivalry with the team dating back to the first three-peat, and the cities had their own rivalry. I think New York Knicks fans could not imagine taking a back seat to Chicago, especially in basketball, which was the New York sport of choice.

We would go to New York, get to Madison Square Garden, and you would not believe the famous people that bordered the court at game time. A bunch of us would sit on the bench and point them out, knowing full well that these famous actors and actresses, singers and comedians had come to see us. Well, they had come to see our team.

There was movie director Spike Lee, of course, but he was a fixture at Knicks games. He was legitimately funny in his comments to us, and his passion was undeniable.

Bill Murray, a native Chicagoan, always seemed to show up in New York. I remember he came to games with his son, Luke, and would talk to us all before the game.

Woody Allen showed up. Alec Baldwin was there with Kim Basinger. John McEnroe was there. We were a hot ticket in New York.

Back in Chicago, we had our local famous fans. John Cusack, the Chicago-raised actor, was around a lot. At the United Center, he was always around back in the hallways by the locker room. I remember once he was filming a movie in Toronto and I ran into him there.

Harold Ramis, the Chicago-based movie director and producer and occasional film star, was a big fan of the Bulls. Actually, he and I became close friends, and we hung out together for a while. He has two boys, Julian and Daniel, and I used to go to his house and just hang around. That was great, because he always got the first cuts of movies that nobody else got to see until they got to the theatres months later.

Jack Nicholson was always around at Lakers games, but he was like Spike Lee was in New York. I remember whenever Phil would call me into a game, I would jump up and run to the scorer's table, and Jack would always tell me to take it easy and save some for the game.

I remember one night when Jerry Seinfeld showed up in Los Angeles. His TV show was at the top of the heap, and he was there to see us.

Penny Marshall, Laverne of *Laverne and Shirley* fame, said she remembered me from my playing days at St. John's.

We met Hootie and the Blowfish, Billy Corrigan from the Smashing Pumpkins, and Eddie Vedder of Pearl Jam, who became a friend of Dennis's. Jimmy Buffett was always there at Miami Heat games. Sylvester Stallone came to a couple of games in Miami.

I was walking around the locker room in New Jersey once and ran into Donald Trump. He had a woman with him, but I am not sure who she was.

Hillary Clinton was raised in a suburb of Chicago, Park Ridge. I remember when she came to the United Center and came into the locker room when her husband was still in office. She talked to everyone, including Dennis, and when she talked to Dennis, he was only wearing a towel. They made the rest of us put on our shirts, our uniform tops, because they didn't want any of us to be topless in front of the First Lady, but of course, Dennis was. He was probably bottomless, too. They would have made an interesting couple.

I wasn't there when President Bill Clinton came into our locker room at the old Capitol Centre in suburban Washington before a game against the Wizards. I was told that was quite a big deal, and he had private time with both Phil and Michael that day.

I did get to meet President Clinton in Washington, when we went to accept congratulations for our 1996 title. I was on crutches at the time, because I tore my plantar fascia, and so was the president. He remarked that my crutches were taller than he was.

Personally, one of the biggest thrills came when I was on a talk show with Harry Teinowitz of the local ESPN radio affiliate in Chicago. I was doing a radio interview, just one of those regular talks I would get into, and at the

We were a media sensation. (Photo courtesy of Bill Wennington)

end of the interview Harry said he had someone who wanted to talk to me.

The voice came on and said, "Hey, Bill, just want to let you know I think you guys are doing great." I was real quiet. I recognized the voice, but I wasn't sure. Harry said, "This is someone you have always wanted to talk to, Bill," and finally I said, "Mr. Dryden?" It was Ken Dryden, who I knew as general manager of the Toronto Maple Leafs. He was my childhood idol when I was growing up when he played goalie for the Montreal Canadiens.

For one of the first times in my life, I was tongue-tied. I got out some sort of remark, "Thank you, sir, you were my idol." I still remember the chill I got out of that.

Bright Lights

We were really an international phenomenon. There were TV reports about children in Africa wearing Bulls T-shirts.

I remember when the playoffs came around in 1996, after we had won 72 regular-season games, suddenly it was like all bets were off in terms of our media coverage. There were Japanese reporters everywhere. There were Chinese reporters. I had reporters and film crews coming from Italy, people I had met when I played in Italy, and they wanted to do interviews in Italian. There was a German crew based in Chicago that was with us all the time. They talked soccer with Toni a lot.

We had two Hispanic stations in Chicago covering us. For a while, Bulls games were broadcast in Spanish in Chicago.

There was a writer for a Polish magazine around all the time. We had a French reporter stationed in Chicago who wrote for multiple publications in his home country.

It was sometimes difficult to conduct interviews with those writers, because their accents were heavy and their English was only so-so. But their English was certainly better than our French, or Japanese, or German, or Spanish.

A Gay Time

After we won the first championship, I took my wife, Anne, out with a friend of mine from Philadelphia, Brian Baldinger, the Fox network broadcaster. We went to the

Chicago establishment Crobar, one of Dennis's favorite late-night hangouts. Dennis had actually arranged for us all to meet there. Eddie Vedder of Pearl Jam was with us, and we had Luc, Steve, Jud, and Jason Caffey. It was a Sunday night, which didn't mean anything to me, but it meant something to Dennis. Sunday night at the Crobar, at least in those days, was Gay Night.

Dennis was ready to make it a special night for all of us.

"Billy, why don't you go up on one of those big boxes and dance a little?" Dennis requested.

I wasn't going to do it, not in a million years, but Dennis somehow got Brian and Anne in on it, and they were urging me on. I think I was finally influenced by the fact that Anne, my always conservative wife who doesn't swear and doesn't drink, was urging me to get up on a big box and dance in front of a predominately homosexual audience.

"Come on, Bill, when are you going to get a chance like this again?"

"Never, I hope," was my reply.

So, with all of my "friends" cheering me on, I got up on one of the dance boxes, started a little bumping and grinding, and Dennis was laughing his head off. Since I was now in character, I took my shirt off, and as soon as I did that, this guy in cowboy boots and a Speedo jumped up on the box and started doing the bump with me.

That, I promise, would not have happened if we weren't celebrating an NBA title.

Playing the Games

One of the great things about being in the NBA is that you get to see the country. When the schedule came out in the summer, and if you were lucky enough to know what team you were playing for that season, you would immediately look to see when the team was going to Los Angeles or San Francisco.

When the league expanded into Florida in 1988, that was great, because that meant trips to Miami, and Michael got to go to Charlotte in his home state of North Carolina. We would be warm in the winter, and that was very important for players from Chicago.

In 1989, the league added Orlando, which meant more warm weather. We also got Minnesota in that expan-

Any time NBA expansion led to games in warm-weather cities was fine by me. (Photo courtesy of Bill Wennington)

sion, so it wasn't all good news. But we had more garden spots to visit.

It was really great for me when the league expanded into Vancouver and Toronto in 1995. Although I am from Montreal, Vancouver is Canada, and it is one of the most beautiful cities in the country. We always seemed to have an extra day there, and because it is part of the Pacific Northwest, it is a terrific city for outdoor activities. In a way, I was back home.

The year we went 72-10 was the first year the NBA expanded into Canada. I remember our first visit to Vancouver. It was one of the last games on our first big west coast road trip. The city was just getting accustomed to being in the National Basketball Association, which was very big for that community, and here we came, the biggest sports story of the year.

We were coming off a big win against Portland, and we were 11-2. We were doing very well, but we were preparing to play an expansion team that had had very little success. There wasn't a lot of tension in the game. It was one of the games we just had to get through. After all, the mighty Bulls should not have much trouble with an expansion team.

However, we got to the fourth quarter of the game, and we were losing, but not by a lot. Derrick Martin, a rookie guard for the Grizzlies at the time, decided to make a statement, and it turned out to be a big mistake.

There was about six minutes left in the game, and we are down by about 16 points, and Derrick started talking trash to Michael.

"You can't guard me, you ain't all that, we are going to beat your butt."

With about 5:30 to go, Michael had had enough. He scored 18 points the rest of the way, and we won by six points, 94-88. At the end of the game, our entire team walked over to Derrick and thanked him for waking Michael up and getting him motivated to play. It was one of the best individual playing explosions I have seen in my basketball life. Michael just willed us to win, and it was Derrick Martin who gave him that will.

Rivalry Talk

By the time 1995-96 rolled around, we had already developed a bit of a rivalry with one of the new franchises, the Orlando Magic. It was the Magic that had beaten us in the playoffs the year before, when Michael came back in March and wasn't quite the Michael Jordan he had been before. Then, early in November of that 95-96 season, Orlando gave us our first loss, 94-88. That was a real blow, a real disappointment, because we were wanting to get back at them for the embarrassment of the previous play-off season. But it somehow reinforced for us what we had to do and had to get done by the end of the season.

As luck would have it, in the playoffs that season, we met Orlando for the Eastern Conference title. We really handled them that year. We won the first game at home by 38 points, and won the first game in Orlando by 17. We won the series 4-0 to go into the championship series against Seattle.

By the time we got to the playoffs that year, Dennis had started changing his hair color and wearing outlandish outfits in public. When we were leaving the Orlando Arena after we won the conference championship that year, there was this guy chasing after the bus, dressed exactly like Dennis. He was a big African-American man with his hair colored bright yellow, with ear piercing and nose piercings and a feather boa. He was wearing leather pants, or maybe they were black spandex, he had a nylon shirt that was skin tight, white, and sunglasses. And he was running after the bus. It was the perfect way to end that series. We all laughed so hard.

It didn't take long for the country to adopt us as America's team. It was probably because Michael was back, and it was only two years since the Bulls had won the first three championships. By the time we got into the playoffs in 1996, we had fans in every stadium in the country. We would go to games where we had more fans than the home team. There would be fans holding up signs in favor of us, and it didn't matter where we were. Jud, Steve, Luc and I would point out the signs to each other, to see if anybody had anything original. I remember "Steve Kerr for President" signs, or "After the game, Jud, let's play volleyball." And there were Bulls jerseys everywhere. It was just unbelievable, and I think it really annoyed some of our opponents, who were trying to beat us before what became a hostile home crowd. But we were America's team. Sorry, guys.

Going for the Record

On April 16, 1996, we were scheduled to play the Milwaukee Bucks, and we were going for our 70th win. That would give us the NBA record for wins in a season, and it was a number that had been hanging around us for months. It was THE topic of conversation on those occasions when Dennis hadn't done something outlandish for a day or two. The record for wins in a season up to that point had been held by the Los Angeles Lakers at 69, and it was set back in 1971-72. It was considered one of those records that wouldn't be broken, and we were about to break it.

We always took a bus up to the Milwaukee, because it is less than an hour and a half from our practice facility in Deerfield, Illinois. We met for the bus around 3:40, and got on just a regular Greyhound bus. We all had our headsets on, expecting the usual bus ride.

But this was different, and we knew so as soon as we got onto Interstate 294 heading north. The first thing we noticed was that there were three helicopters following us. They were from news stations, and they were covering our trip up to Milwaukee.

Then we noticed that whenever we would go under an overpass, there were people standing on the road above us, displaying banners draped down over the side of the overpass. There would be like 20 to 100 people standing on every overpass, waving signs. "We love you, Michael," "We love you, Scottie," "We love you, Dennis." You could see their cars parked along the side of the road. They were waiting to get a glimpse of our bus as it took us on the way to history.

The helicopters followed us all the way to the Bradley Center. It was surreal.

We Lost?

On our second long road trip west that season in late January and early February, we hit a bump in the road. We played a game against Denver, and we somehow found ourselves trailing by 32 points early in the second half. I remember I had 21 points in that game. We fought back and ended up losing by six points, and it was really a close game at the end, but we couldn't get it done all the way.

Then, two nights later, we lost to Phoenix. We were really disappointed by that. It was the only time that year that we lost consecutive games, and it was really kind of surprising to us.

The all-star break came right after that, and I think those losses helped remind us of what we needed to do to pull things together.

It's funny how everything worked out in that case. We went away thinking, "We are good, but maybe we are not as good as we thought." I know it's a cliché, but it really was a wake-up call for us. We did not lose two games in a row the rest of that season.

Miami Heated

We had a rivalry with the Miami Heat, but it wasn't really the players' rivalry. The rivalry belonged to our coach, Phil Jackson, who had a personal nemesis in Miami Heat coach Pat Riley. The two men, obviously among the most talented coaches in NBA history, could not stop sending sometimes innocent and sometimes nasty jibes at each other through the media. It started when Riley was

Dennis Rodman always kept things interesting when he played against Alonzo Mourning. (AP/WWP)

coaching the New York Knicks, and the Bulls that won the first three championships had a tremendous rivalry with that team.

By the time we got to the second three-peat, Riley had moved on to Miami. Whenever a Miami game was coming up, the papers were filled with little digs Jackson and Riley would make at each other. I'm sure each coach was using it as motivation for his respective team, but there was always something there, and our games became huge affairs as a result. The tension at Bulls-Miami games were very similar to what it was like when we would play New York in the Garden.

One big difference between the Bulls-Knicks rivalry and the Bulls-Heat rivalry was that there was a tension between two players in the Chicago-Miami series that didn't exist in the Chicago-New York series. Dennis Rodman, our power forward, and Alonzo Mourning, Miami's scowling center, had a relationship that had to be witnessed to be believed.

When you watched Dennis play, you only considered his physical skills, his ability to get to the rebounds, and his way of playing defense. But Dennis was really smart, and he played a psychological game with our opponents, who didn't know quite what to think about playing against Dennis Rodman.

That was most evident when we played Miami. Dennis got inside the head of Alonzo Mourning so much that Mourning would often forget about playing basketball all together. Dennis did the same thing to Karl Malone of the Utah Jazz.

It would become a contest of wills between Dennis and Alonzo. Dennis knew that once he got a player thinking about him instead of about the team, that player would become less effective at playing the game.

Phil and Pat

Phil was a forward, Pat was a guard. Phil was cerebral, Pat was stylish. Phil was coaching Chicago, Pat was coaching New York first and then Miami. The two men just didn't see eye to eye.

I'm not sure why they disliked each other so much, but it certainly came out in the newspapers any time we played a Pat Riley team. I don't remember the specific taunts, but I do remember sitting in the locker room talking about it and laughing. Phil called the Knicks thugs, Pat mocked Phil's intellect and his attempt to manipulate the media.

For us, I think we all knew each coach was just trying to set a stage for fans, the league and the referees. Whether they actually hated each other, I don't really know.

I do know that when Phil used the media to get a message across, he was up to something. With Phil, things always had more than one level. Phil rarely spoke off the cuff. There was always a lot of planning behind what he said.

Maybe he just thought he could push Pat's buttons.

How You Doing?

Dennis used to pat Mourning on the butt, and Mourning did not know what to make of that. Dennis was always being playful about his sexuality in public, dressing up in a wedding gown on that one occasion, and dressing like something out of *The Rocky Horror Picture Show*. So when Dennis would pat Mourning on the butt, it really drove Mourning up a wall. Mourning would slap Dennis's hand away, and Dennis would give Mourning a sly smile, and Mourning was very obviously freaked out.

Dennis also enjoyed the fact people were talking about him. Part of Dennis's act was that people didn't know what he was all about. Dennis thrived on getting guys unmotivated to play, where they were worrying about all those little side issues he kept bringing up.

The one thing Dennis did on the floor that was maybe not necessary was when he head-butted referee Ted Bernhardt. I think he thought about it before he did it, but I don't think he was thinking about it AS he did it. I think he looked at the guy and said to himself, "Maybe I will give him a little bump." It was more of a heat of the moment kind of thing. Dennis got a lot of bad calls on him because of his reputation, and I think it all just boiled over at that moment.

Dennis and the Boys

Dennis just kind of knew which guys didn't want to be touched unnecessarily, and Dennis would then go out of his way to invade their space.

The butt pat is part of sports, but with Dennis, you had to wonder if it took on a different meaning. After all, this is a guy who appeared in New York in a wedding dress, complete with a veil.

When we played the Indiana Pacers in the seven-game Eastern Conference final in 1998, Dennis went to new lengths to get his opponent out of his game. His opponent in matchups was Antonio Davis, who I got to know when he played for the Bulls years later.

Antonio told me about the time Dennis got tangled up with him, sort of tried to disentangle, but then just took him by the arm and danced with him, waltz style. "He was touching me and always poking me and grabbing me," Antonio said. "Then we got in a foul situation and he grabbed me and started dancing with me, and that was it. I was ready to go right then, but I kept my head because I knew he was trying to get me to commit a technical foul."

Dennis was always pushing the limits to try to get guys out of their game.

CHAPTER NINE

Reading Material

The Bulls always went on a west coast trip in the middle of November, about two weeks into the start of the season, because the circus was scheduled to appear at the United Center. We had to go twice a year, but the first trip was always a little hard because it came right after the season started. It also almost always included a road trip Thanksgiving Day, and the team would have to scramble to find something that felt like a Thanksgiving dinner.

For a poor team, such a trip so early in the season would be considered a hardship. For us, it was a time to get out and knock off some teams, get some road wins, start establishing ourselves as a dominant team. Phil Jackson saw it as a bonding time, and with it being so early, we got a chance to bond early, which had benefit as the season progressed.

Before I got there, Phil had made a bit of a name for himself in NBA circles by handing out books for everyone to read on the west coast trips. Phil Jackson was well known as an intellectual, at least in basketball circles, and he did believe in trying to help us grow as people beyond our basketball lives. I think that is one reason he gave us all reading material to occupy our sometimes long and lonely hours on the two-week trips west.

I think he also wanted to give the players something to do on the road as a viable option to going out, staying out late and carousing. He figured if he gave us each a book, we might actually read it, improve ourselves, and make better use of our down time on the road. If a book actually kept us out of trouble, even for a night, all the better.

The books weren't always enlightening, academic, philosophical books. All the books he gave me were murder-mystery types, or adventure-type books. He tried to reach out to us as he saw fit, and he wanted to hand out books that might actually get opened up, even by the non-readers in the group.

I remember when Toni first came to the United States, he spoke broken English and didn't read English well, so Phil gave him a comic book. It was something he could read. Whether Toni read it, or anyone read their books, I don't know. I know I read mine, and Steve Kerr read his.

We would get on the plane to head out west and Phil would make a walk through the plane handing out books. When he got done, we would all compare with each other what we got.

"Did you get a big one?"

"How come you got such a small one?"

Everyone on the team got one, and that included Michael. Even guys who just joined the team would get a book. It was a part of the Bulls legend.

I remember that Phil gave Dennis the book *Zen and the Art of Motorcycle Maintenance* one year. He thought Dennis would be intrigued by the title, I guess. But, you know what, now that I think about it, I think he gave me that book once, too. Maybe we all got that one.

Phil made thoughtful choices in the reading material. He inscribed each book. He didn't write anything particularly revealing, but he gave a lot of thought to the choices.

I asked him about it one time.

"How did you know I would like these books?'

"We talk," he said. "I thought about it, and I decided you were the type who would enjoy the challenge of a book of this nature."

I remember one year he gave me a Jonathan Kellerman book. I couldn't read it. It was too out there. I tried, and I got about halfway through, but I couldn't finish it. So Phil missed on that one.

More on Books

The one book Phil gave me that I really enjoyed was *Dirty White Boys* by Stephen Hunter. It's a suspense story about guys who break out of prison. I also liked one of the Tony Hillerman's he gave me called *The First Eagle*.

I don't know what Phil was trying to say with the choice of books he gave me. There was a always a criminal element to the story, but I think that might have been coincidental.

Past History

Getting a pass from Michael was acceptance from Michael. One of my first as a teammate of Michael's turned out to be one of the big moments in my career, from a personal standpoint.

Michael and I had a short history of playing together before we became Bulls teammates. We played together on the McDonalds' All-America team in 1981. We were high school seniors, playing in an All-Star atmosphere before heading off to college.

The way that game went, I would get the defensive rebound, throw the ball to Michael at halfcourt, he would go down and score. I only had four rebounds, but I had 12 assists. I threw them all to Michael so he could score.

I think Michael respects personal history more so than anyone else I had seen before. In 1981, we were all high school kids, and we weren't sure how it was all going to end up for us. He didn't really start to shine until his second year at North Carolina. We were sitting around with Chris Mullin and Patrick Ewing, and we were talking about what was going to happen, talking about schools, who is going to win championships, whether St. John's was going to be good, or North Carolina. Once we became teammates, Michael mentioned that day to me once. I think that little bit of personal history, that past relationship, that one very pleasant conversation, helped me in my professional relationship with Michael Jordan.

New York Moment

In the spring of 1995, Michael Jordan came back from his first retirement. I was finally going to get my chance to play with him in the pros. It just came about two years after I thought it was going to happen, which was back in the summer of 1993 when I joined the Bulls and just before Michael retired.

Michael practiced with us for about two weeks, although he had been working out in town for months. It was decided his first game back would be in Indianapolis against the Pacers, which was probably both good news and bad news for them. They could certainly sell more tickets, although the Bulls were already a pretty popular ticket in Indianapolis. The bad news is that the media attention for that game was huge, out of control, and the Pacers had to deal with that.

We lost that game in overtime but won at Boston in our next game. Michael's first home game that spring was against Orlando, and we lost that game, which might have been an indication of how our playoff series against them was going to go that year.

After a game in Atlanta, we had three days before we played in New York. It was Michael's return to Madison Square Garden, where he had burned the Knicks so many times in the past. In their first three championship years, the Bulls beat the Knicks in the playoffs all three times to advance in the postseason tournament. New York had a love-hate relationship with Michael, and here he was, coming back.

It was a big deal, a huge deal. The media attention was higher than ever. The building was electric, thick with humanity and anticipation.

Michael Jordan's return to NY was a big deal. (Photo courtesy of Bill Wennington)

Michael loves a big stage, and on that night, March 28, 1995, he scored 55 points, far beyond his best scoring outburst so far that season. In those previous four games, his best had been 32 points. It was as if he wanted to prove that he was that player again, the one who could put up 50 points and win.

But the game was close. We were tied late, and there was a timeout. I had just gotten into the game a few minutes earlier because Luc Longley had fouled out. Phil drew up a play for Michael, of course, because we were in New York, Michael was having his first big night out, and it just figured Michael would want to hit the winning shot.

The play drawn up was one we had already run 100 times in practice. It was a play out of the triangle, because all of our plays were out of the triangle.

In the triangle, players are required to make judgment calls. It is why the triangle really needs smart basketball players to succeed. The triangle tells you to go where the defense isn't.

On the last play of the New York game, I was on the weak side, clearing out of the post so Michael could drive to the basket. Patrick Ewing was guarding me, but he left me to step in front of Michael and fill the void. Charles Oakley was behind me, guarding somebody else out on the wing. When Patrick left me, I did what I was supposed to do. I stepped to the basket. Michael saw me wide open and hit me with the pass, surprising everyone in Madison Square Garden. I dunked the ball for my only basket and we were up by two points with three seconds to go, 113-111.

I wasn't surprised to get the pass. It was just good basketball. We had run plays like that in practice. I knew Michael trusted me. We had played together on occasion coming out of college. He knew I would do what I was supposed to do on that play. Michael wants to win, and when he sees the opportunity to win a game, whether he is taking the shot or passing the ball, he will do what it takes to win. He is going to give everybody an opportunity to do his job.

It was great for me. People still talk to me about it when I am in New York. I loved it, since I played college basketball in New York, and had played plenty of games in Madison Square Garden. New York was always fun for me. I had a lot of family there for that game.

Michael's return to NY was a big deal.

Winning Number 1,
(or was it Number 4?)

After we won 72 games in the 1995-96 regular season, it was clear we were going to be the favorite to win the title. We swept the Washington Wizards in the first round, beat the Atlanta Hawks 4-1 in the second round and crushed the Miami Heat 4-1 in the Eastern Conference Finals.

We were playing the Seattle SuperSonics in the championship, and nobody gave the SuperSonics much of a chance to beat us. We won the first two games at home, and won the third game by a blowout score of 108-86, going up 3-0. But we lost the next two games in Seattle, both by pretty good scores, and everyone was disappointed to be going home with just a 3-2 lead in the best-of-seven series.

We were leaving the Key Arena after that fifth game, and Michael came on the bus with a smile on his face and a cigar in his mouth.

"Don't worry, fellas, we are winning the next one. I guarantee you."

We won Game 6 by 12 points, 87-75, and I remember as it was winding down, thinking about what it meant to be winning an NBA championship.

My family was there at the United Center, my wife and my son, my mother-in-law, my parents.

You are always told not to celebrate before the game is over, but it was apparent we were going to win. We were high-fiving each other on the bench. When the final buzzer sounded, there was mayhem at the United Center, but the emotion I recall more than any other was relief. There was such a release of emotion, that you had accom-

The Grant Park celebrations were awesome. (Photo courtesy of Bill Wennington)

plished something you had been trying to accomplish for so long.

There are times when you come close to winning and don't do it, and here we were, the champions. We had done it. I couldn't stop yelling. I was hoarse for three days.

It was a non-stop blast. You might go to sleep for a little while, but then you would get a phone call from someone on the team. Even after it was over, I saw a lot of the guys. We couldn't get enough of the celebration.

I didn't go to bed until 8 a.m. the day after the winning game, and I probably slept only three hours because we had celebrating to do the next day.

In the Park

Part of the tradition of winning in Chicago with the Bulls was the Grant Park celebrations. We didn't have parades, like the one the Bears had when they won the Super Bowl in 1986. Instead, the city gathered the team at the bandshell in Grant Park in downtown Chicago, so the party had a central location.

Of course, I got to go to three Grant Park celebrations, but the first one we did in 1996 was amazing. When we got up on stage, all you could see was people. There were people in the trees, and people as far as you could see. That was phenomenal.

We met as a team at the Berto Center, received our championship T-shirts and hats, and we were allowed to bring our families, so there were wives and kids running around. We were put in a bus and traveled down to Grant Park.

Once we got there, we were herded into a reception area downstairs at the bandshell, where they had some drinks and some food. We were waiting to go on stage, and it actually got kind of hot down there. Luckily, we didn't have to wait too long, and once we got on stage, the electricity of the moment was almost unbearable. Everyone was there to see us, to thank us, to congratulate us, and to be a part of what we did.

The Second Time Around

After that incredible summer of 1996, the next season came very quickly. We didn't have much time off, and what time we had, we filled up with celebrating our championship victory. We were the toast of the sporting world, and that status can occupy a lot of your time.

We weren't much different, roster-wise, for the 1996-97 season. We had Robert Parish instead of James Edwards as the third center, and Jack Haley was no longer needed to serve as Dennis's best friend and hand-holder. We were almost identical to the 1995-96 team, and we were looking at another 70-win season. We knew that it would be very difficult to accomplish, that the rest of the league would be gunning for us in a different manner, but we were pretty confident that we were the best team in the league.

We didn't manage to win 70 games that season. We finished 69-13, and of course, the talk started as soon as the season ended that the Bulls had already gotten too old. It was kind of ridiculous. Sixty-nine wins was the NBA record before we won 72 games the year before. It was kind of hard to understand, except that writers have to have something to write. They couldn't write that we were just as good as the year before, because we hadn't dominated quite like we did the year before.

Anyway, I know why we didn't win 70 games that season. I was hurt for a lot of the season and didn't play. I tore my plantar fascia in early April, and missed all of those critical games at the end. Can't win without me.

Actually, the Bulls brought in Brian Williams to play center right after I got hurt. He played well and was very popular in town. He was obviously very smart and great

The second title was frustrating because I couldn't play and had to hobble to the White House ceremony. (AP/WWP)

with the quip. When properly motivated, he played strong around the basket.

Just as remarkable as winning an NBA title was seeing your team win the NBA title without your contribution. I was on the outside looking in throughout that playoff season. I knew all along I wasn't on the inside. I was an outsider on my own team. I was at practice, and I could survey the atmosphere around the team, but I wasn't really involved like I had been the year before. It was sort of painful.

Sometimes, it might seem like guys who aren't playing have it easy, but when you win, there is no satisfaction in not playing. That's kind of the way I felt about the second championship. I wasn't in there when the games really counted.

The 1997 Finals

We played Utah in the finals that year. We felt confident going out to Utah, but we knew Karl Malone and John Stockton had given us trouble in the past. However, Dennis brought his game to a new level at that point, and became a focal point of the Utah mindset.

Like he did to Alonzo Mourning, Dennis started slapping Karl on the butt and getting inside his head. You could see Karl lose his composure trying to deal with Dennis. Karl Malone was not one to put up with such tomfoolery. He was Serious Basketball Man. Dennis was Insane Basketball Freak. The two men did not mesh.

That was the year the media selected Malone as the league's Most Valuable Player over Michael. Even the three Chicago beat writers had voted for Malone. Michael told them he understood their selection, that Malone had had a great year and that voting for Michael was boring, but I think he used it as a motivational tool.

I had never seen such determination in anyone as Michael had that playoff season.

I remember the game in Salt Lake City in which Michael played sick. Before the game, he was chalky white, with a 103- 104-degree fever, lying down in the training room. We all could see him, and we wondered if he was going to be able to play. But John Ligmanowski, our equipment manager, told us we were going to win. We told him we thought Michael was going to die, but John said whenever he is sick, he plays harder and better.

He played his heart out that night, but whenever the whistle blew to stop play, you could see his shoulders slump, and he went into standby mode, trying to stay afloat. When the whistle blew again, he would suck it up, stand straight and get back out there.

When the game was over, he was hooked up to an IV almost immediately because he was so dehydrated. It was cool, in a weird way, because he was so sick, and I know most people would be in bed, moaning, and he was out on the floor willing us to win. It was one of the most phenomenal things I had seen in basketball.

We won the championship that year on Steve Kerr's foul-line jumper, and I was so happy for my good friend. Despite all the pressure we faced, we had done it again. We were NBA champions for a second season in a row.

The Last Dance

We were 62-20 in 1997-98, and it was all Joe Kleine's fault.

At the beginning of that year, you could see it wasn't going to be like the two previous years. It took guys a little longer to get back in the swing of things. We had gone to Paris for a tournament in October of that year, and we had to come back in early for training because of it. That trip was fun, but it took a lot of energy, and we all suffered jet lag. It was difficult, and it caused us trouble as the season began.

When that season started, when we got our playbooks, on the cover it said "The Last Dance". Phil was determined to get out of Chicago after that season, because his relationship with Jerry Krause was completely over.

We saw "The Last Dance" and I think we all knew it was over.

Phil told us to enjoy the season, stop and smell the roses, see what is going on around you, because this is it, it is not going to happen again after this year. "I am not going to come back," he told us.

We knew what we had to do. That was a bit of a shock. We got off to a rocky start, and worked hard to get the focus. Everybody had settled into their roles, and Dennis was full-blown Dennis by this time, getting more and more involved in creating a media blitz stir.

We were not as dominating as we had been and when we got into the Eastern Conference finals against Indiana, some people gave the Pacers a shot at beating us. They took us to a seventh game, tied 3-3 in the series, but all of their wins were in Indianapolis. They had not come close to beating us in Chicago, and they couldn't do it in the last game, losing 88-83. We were going to the title game again.

Dealing with the Pacers

In all of the Bulls' championship runs, there was only one seven-game series, and that was a second-round matchup with New York in 1992, I think. The Bulls had never been forced into a Game 7 in either the conference finals or the NBA Finals.

In 1998, everyone thought the Bulls were ripe for an upset. We had had a contentious season, everybody knew the team was going to get broken up at season's end, and Dennis was coming more and more unraveled. The Pacers took advantage of all of that to give us a terrific battle in the Eastern Conference final.

The key to that series was not our offense but our defense, and as always, our defensive structure was built around Scottie more than Michael. Just like he did back in 1991 with Magic Johnson, Scottie was assigned to disrupt Mark Jackson of the Pacers, and Scottie made it very hard for the Pacers to get into their patterned offense as a result.

All the games in that series were won by the home team. After all the hype that went into us being forced to a Game 7, we were pretty confident we would win at the United Center, and it turned out to be a game we had in hand for much of the fourth quarter.

I remember again that the media thought if we could be forced into a Game 7 in the conference finals, we could be in real trouble in the finals. But that year, the series against Utah seemed even less dramatic and tense than the one the year before.

The Indiana series actually prepared us for the finals. It served as a wake-up call and made us realize we had two more weeks to play to get to where we wanted to be.

We won that series in six games, and I know people were disappointed we didn't win at home in five. But we felt in control the entire time, and when Michael hit the shot with his hand extended, all of our faith was rewarded.

Here's a story I haven't thought about in a long time.

After we won the 1998 NBA Finals in Salt Lake City, we bussed back to our hotel, and we were just going to get on a plane and go home rather than spend another night in Utah. So we got our clothes from our rooms and got onto a bus at the hotel, with thousands of fans standing outside the hotel property cheering us.

Michael was the last one on the bus, and when he got on, he popped open one of the emergency exits on top of the bus, and got up on the roof of the bus. He was standing there cheering with the fans, and he was like a little kid, in a way I hadn't seen him act before. Michael had already been through the championship routine five times before that, but he was enjoying that one like it was his first. Maybe he was enjoying it like it was his last.

I have a video of his feet hanging down into the bus as he was getting up onto the roof or down from there. I remember thinking what a neat moment that was, for him, for us and for the fans. You could see the release of the pressure that we were living with. It was just a cool moment, and of course, it was one of the last.

Utah Again?

We did not have homecourt advantage for that finals. I think we were favored to win, but not by much. I think there were a lot of people who thought Utah was going to do it.

Some of the similarities between the first three-peat and the second three-peat were eerie. The Bulls had homecourt advantage for the Finals in 1991 and 1992 but not in 1993. We had homecourt advantage for the Finals in 1996 and 1997 but not in 1998.

Of course, the most memorable moment from that finals was the final moment. Michael Jordan moved Bryon Russell out of his way and hit that 18-foot jumper to win the game. He stood with his arm extended for the longest time, freezing that image in all of our memories. If it was to be his last shot, it was quite a last shot to take.

That was a different celebration than we had the first time. We were away from home, nobody was around. Our

wives were there, but there wasn't the same group of people that had been with us in Chicago the previous year,
hanging out in our locker room after the game. It wasn't as
intense in Utah. It was pretty much the team, although I
did get to douse Carmen Electra with water, because she
was there hanging out with Dennis. Leonardo DiCaprio
was there, too, for some reason. And that was it.

No More Dancing

I guess we knew, even as we were celebrating, that it
was over, over. There was a glimmer of hope that we might
have another year. We knew Phil was planning to leave,
and we thought Michael wouldn't come back if Phil wasn't
here. But it was hard to imagine that a three-time championship team would not come together again for one more
run.

After that game we went to the hotel, packed our bags
and left that night. There was no partying in Salt Lake
City, or Park City. We took off for home right after the
game. We did celebrate on the plane, but we were all very
tired that night.

We got to our landing area at O'Hare and there were
thousands of people at the airport waiting for us.

We had valets move our cars so we could get out of
there. We all got into our vehicles and went home. It was
all so much more subdued.

A couple of days later, we gathered again at the Berto
Center to head down to Grant Park. We all knew at that
moment that we were going to be having our last celebration.

Michael didn't even join us at the Berto Center for the trip downtown. He was already there, handling some sort of business, and he met us at the park. It was all so much different. The Beatles were breaking up.

The Media

We were the biggest sports story in the world, and the world was watching us. Somebody told me we had more reporters following us on a daily basis than were following the president of the United States.

Once we got going in 1996, the media contingent was huge, and in every city a new group of reporters, broadcasters and television types came around to talk to us, asking us the same questions we had heard so many times before.

But we had the core group of media members that traveled with us everywhere we went. We had the broadcasters—Neil Funk, Tom Dore, Wayne Larrivee, Johnny "Red" Kerr and John Paxson—who were able to travel with us on our plane, because they were team employees. The newspaper guys—Kent McDill of the *Daily Herald*, Terry Armour of the *Chicago Tribune*, and John Jackson of the *Chicago Sun-Times*—were friendly faces in the crowd of reporters who invaded our personal space on a daily basis.

In professional sports, there are always reporters who are trying to make a name for themselves, to get the scoop, the big story, to tell the negative aspects of the very positive life we were leading. It is difficult to be around guys when you don't know what they are going to write. In my previous stops in the NBA, there really wasn't a lot of trust involved.

When I was playing with the Sacramento Kings, long before my Bulls' adventure, Marty McNeal of the *Sacramento Bee* was a great guy, the one good guy following us in Sacramento. The other guys, you just couldn't be sure what they would write. You didn't know what would happen if they happened to see you drinking a beer or a glass of wine the night before a game. If you had a bad game the next night, you had to wonder if the writer would mention your drinking from the night before in his story.

When I came to Chicago, a relationship already existed between the media and the team, from covering all of the previous championships. For the most part, the reporters were covering a winning program, and the goal for most reporters was to find a unique way to tell what was becoming an historic story. When teams are winning, there isn't a lot of negative stuff to write.

The beat writers were guys we saw every day. They either stayed in the same hotel as we did, or stayed close by. We would see them in restaurants or shopping centers.

We knew what they were writing about us, even if we didn't read it ourselves, and we knew what was on the record and what was off.

Not a lot of athletes would tell you this, but it was comforting to know you could trust a reporter. If you are always looking over your shoulder at what they are doing, it is definitely uncomfortable.

Faces for TV (Except for Tom)

The television play-by-play guys were Wayne Larivee and Tom Dore. They worked for competing networks that shared our broadcast rights, and Tom was around more often than Wayne was. Wayne always had a lot of other assignments he was running off to.

Tom and I had a good relationship. He was a former center, two inches taller as I was, and so we had that in common. He offered me advice on my plans to get into broadcasting when I was done playing.

Neil Funk was the play-by-play man for the radio broadcasts. He has been around the league forever. He started in Kansas City, I think, went to Philadelphia, went to New Jersey, went back to Philly, then came to Chicago.

Neal has a great voice, knows the game, and understands what is going on behind the scenes. He has a great sense of humor and was a fun guy to be around. He started the phrase ka-ka-ka-boom for three-pointers. A lot of people experienced the Bulls' championships through his voice.

Johnny "Red" Kerr was the color commentator for television. He was the Bulls' first coach, back in the late 1960s, and he was one of the league's classic big men. When he, Tom and I work together on Bulls games, we have to represent one of the tallest broadcast teams in NBA history.

Johnny and I would talk about basketball, but the thing about Red was that he would never approach you to tell you something about your game. He would wait until his advice was solicited. I always respected that as a player. You have enough people telling you what you should do.

Johnny "Red" Kerr (left) was a member of the Bulls family. (Photo courtesy of Bill Wennington)

He would always say, "What I like to do," in describing a play, rather than, "This is what you should do."

When I came to Chicago, Johnny and his wife, Betsy, were very supportive of my wife and me. They were very open to Anne and me, took us in and made us feel comfortable.

After he got done playing, and after one year as an assistant coach, John Paxson became the color commentator on radio, teaming up with Neal Funk. John was great at that job, because you knew from the moment he started that he knew the game. He played for so long, and had been a part of what we were going through, only he did it a few years earlier. You could talk to him about anything. He was almost an extension of the coaches. He knew the system we were playing and the instructions we were receiving from the coaching staff. He knew the league and really knew the players in the league. We all already had a relationship with him as a teammate and as a coach, and it just continued on as he worked behind the microphone.

Those men all helped me out tremendously with the start of my broadcast career. They made it very easy for me.

It sound a little corny, but throughout our championship run, it felt like the entire operation was being run by a family. Your brothers and sisters were the team members and staff, your parents were the coaches and your cousins were the media. It was great traveling around the country with those people.

Transitions

It seemed like the entire three-year run of championships had one difficult constant running through, or more like under, our little party. We never knew for sure how long we were going to stay together.

Phil Jackson and Michael Jordan were dealing with contract issues on an annual basis. Scottie Pippen was never happy with his contract status. And we never knew when Dennis Rodman would be called back to his home planet.

With every excitement, there was concern. Every win brought us closer to our demise. We were the best team in the world, and we were tense because someone or something was trying not to defeat us, but to destroy us.

After the 1995-96 title, the first one for many of us, the stories started that Phil Jackson had had enough. He was going to retire. He was thinking we weren't ever going to get any better than the 72-10 team he had just coached, and he might as well get out while the getting was good.

There weren't any more positives to be gained from continuing. His relationships within the organization were strained, especially his relationship with general manager Jerry Krause, and he was getting tired of it.

I think every single member of the team found time that summer to visit with Phil to try to convince him to come back for the 1996-97 season. I know I talked to him, and I know the guys I was closest to made a similar effort. We all told him we could do it again, and we wanted to. We all begged him to stay. He responded to that kind of outpouring of faith, I think. He stayed, and we won the 1996-97 title.

Michael Jordan was operating on a series of one-year contracts at that time, and he had publicly tied his future to that of Phil. No Phil, no Michael. It was a testy atmosphere for each of our summers.

After the '97 title, I think Phil felt we could win it again in 1997-98, and that having two sets of three-peats would make for some nice symmetry. But he made it very clear to us all that the 1997-98 season was going to be our last.

The Second Jerry

I always had a good relationship with Jerry Krause, the Bulls' general manager. He was the man who brought me in to the team in 1993, although I was never quite sure whether it was he or Phil who was most responsible for adding me to the roster. Jerry had many quirks, but I respected him as a person and as a general manager. I think he was a great judge of talent, and did a wonderful job finding the players who could work together as a team around Michael and Scottie.

Did Jerry do some things that were different, and that bothered people? Did he have relationship problems with people? Yeah, he did. But it takes all kinds of people to make things work. And I think his poor relationship with Phil actually helped us as a team.

In one way, Phil used Jerry as a unifying tool. He channeled our efforts and our talents as a unit, and he used our testy relationship with Jerry as a motivating factor. If Jerry Krause wasn't our general manager, and Phil didn't have that contentious relationship with him, he would have had to find another motivational tool to use.

That being said, I consider Jerry Krause a friend, and I think he did a great job as general manager of the Bulls.

If the coaches were our parents, as I suggested before, maybe Jerry was the grandfather.

Jeering Jerry

Maybe it is natural to dislike the man who signs your checks, and thus it made sense for Phil to dislike Jerry Krause so much. I don't know if there was more to it than that, but Jerry made himself such a target for verbal abuse and taunts, that it seemed like the way things were going to go with the Bulls.

Jerry had the knack of saying the wrong things at the wrong time, and he tried to share credit for things we were doing on the floor. But I think the problems with Phil and Jerry started way before I got there.

I do know the team resented the fact Jerry always came on that first West Coast trip every year. We felt he was around too much. It was always at least 10 days, and there was no escaping him when he was on the bus with us every day.

Add to that Jerry's personality quirk. He was going to be secretive and, if not dishonest, he would not be totally honest with you. He hid facts and confused conversations to keep his little secrets.

Finally, his physical attributes made him an easy target and was used as a motivational tool.

I really think the Phil and Jerry problem came down to a control issue. Phil wanted to have more control over everything that was going on, and Jerry was not going to let him in. Phil wanted to be in charge, the way he was in Los Angeles with the Lakers.

The Third Head

During the first three-peat, the Bulls had what became known as the three-headed monster at center. Most of the time, it was Bill Cartwright, Will Perdue, and Stacey King, with Scott Williams in the mix when someone was injured.

When we got around to the second three-peat, my three-peat, the three-headed monster was a little more flexible. It was Luc Longley, me and some other tall guy who was at the end of his career.

There is a basketball saying that size can't be coached. We had the benefit of about 21 feet of real estate and 18 fouls to use against the better centers in the league. We were playing Shaquille O'Neal, Rik Smits and Patrick Ewing most years, and in a seven-game series, it was beneficial to have three centers to go to, in case one of us got beat up or in foul trouble early.

Luc was the big body inside, the starter most of the time. He was the best defender in the middle. I was the guy who ran better than most centers, could pull out for a shot to get the defender out of the middle, making room for Michael and Scottie to operate inside. The third guy was filling a role as the 12th man on the bench. They all got their time to play, and they helped us win.

Three Heads Are Better

In the 1995-96 season, James Edwards was brought in. He had made his name as part of the Bad Boys in Detroit, and he came to us at the end of his career. He had a big body, which helped when it was time for us to try to play O'Neal, especially.

In 1996-97, it was Robert Parish, a very special addition for Jerry Krause, who had befriended Parish early in his career. Parish had made his name with the Boston Celtics, and had several championships before he got to us. For a big man, Robert was very limber, loose, pliable. He helped me figure out how I could be more nimble. He was into karate and tae kwan do. That is probably why he played for as long as he did. He was always loose, physically. I got a little more conscientious about stretching before a game once I saw him prepare.

Joe Kleine was with us in 1997-98. The strength coaches, Erik Helland and Al Vermiel, loved him. He was a monster, muscular. He was what Erik called a "nice spec-imen." You couldn't push your way through him on the floor. He was coming in at the tail end of his career, but he hadn't won a title. He had been on the Olympic team with Michael back in the early 1980s, when it was still college kids. He was excited about the possibility of being on an NBA championship team, but he didn't make the playoff roster that year, which was a disappointment for him.

CHAPTER TEN

Practical Jokes

I think one reason people become professional athletes is because it allows them to avoid growing up all the way. It's a Peter Pan existence, at least when we are playing the games. The adult world enters only when we get involved in business decisions, like contract hassles.

But for the most part, we were adults getting paid a huge amount of money to play a kid's game, and we took advantage of the fact that we didn't have parents around telling us to put our toys away.

There were times we acted like the kids we had always been.

We pulled practical jokes on each other, and we had our classics. Dennis Rodman liked to put sports analgesic creams in guys' underwear. John Ligmanowski, our equipment manager, was big on the frozen underwear.

Players would hide shoes, street shoes usually, and we got into a thing where we were putting offensive bumper stickers on each other's cars. I remember we had bumper stickers proclaiming appreciation of the musical group Wham!, the band George Michael was in, and we would stick those on cars in the quiet moments. No one wanted to be seen in a car with a "We Love Wham" bumper sticker.

I enjoyed the practical jokes, but I didn't get really inventive until circumstances forced me to make a practical joke statement.

Erik Helland was the assistant strength coach at the time. He is a hunter, and one time he drilled out the hanging bar in my locker, and filled it with cotton balls covered in fox urine. It smelled up the entire locker room. It wasn't a horrible smell, but it wasn't nice, either.

We spent a month trying to figure out where it was coming from. I had the cleaning crew go over my locker three times with disinfectant, because it was obviously coming from my area. Steve Kerr and Jud Buechler were in on the joke, and they were always on me to clean out my stuff, wash my clothes again, that sort of thing. We each had two lockers at the Berto Center, one with a door that closed and one that was open, and I couldn't use my good locker because of the smell.

Eventually, I figured out Erik was responsible, and I had to get him back.

I spent $600 at one of those mail-it-yourself stores on those packing peanuts, the ones that are so hard to deal with once you open a package.

One night, after we returned from a road trip, I went back and forth between my garage and the Berto Center six times to get all of those packages of peanuts into the Berto Center. I filled his office, from floor to ceiling, with the things. I also put them in his locker in the coach's locker room.

Erik came into work early the next morning, around 6 a.m. He was feeling ill that day, with a 102 fever, and he wanted to check his messages early, hoping he could get some rest before practice started.

I came into practice at 8:30, an hour earlier than usual, just to see what Erik had done, and he had already cleaned out his entire office. We had interns working there with the team, and they did most of the work. There were all sorts of garbage bags outside the Berto Center filled with those Styrofoam nuts.

Erik was livid at me. He wouldn't talk to me, except to call me some names.

After practice, he came up to me and congratulated me, telling me I had successfully gotten back at him. We were even, he said.

He told me he was going to go get dressed to work out, and I realized he hadn't found the peanuts in his locker. So he went into the coach's room, and all of a sudden I hear him yelling. He was mad at me all over again.

Al Vermeil, the head strength coach, told me it was wrong to get involved with Erik in that way. I thought he was giving me parental advice, but he was actually warning me that Erik had so much idle time between workouts with the players that he would be able to get back at me much easier than I could.

The frozen underwear was exactly what it sounds like. Guys take off their dress clothes and get in basketball gear. John Ligmanowski would take the underwear, soak it, freeze it, and then hang it back up so that it looked like it did when it was hung up originally. You would reach for it and then find out quickly that Ligmanowski had too much free time, too.

Hot Pants

Dennis was big into the Ben-Gay in your underwear. That was a trick that was effective and mean-spirited.

We were in Washington, D.C. and Dennis did it to Jud Buechler and Steve Kerr. He wanted to do it to Luc Longley, but I talked him out of that because Luc and I had a nonaggression pact. We agreed to let each other know if we were the target of a practical joke, and to wave off the offenders when possible.

But Dennis wasn't exactly subtle with his trick. He liked to use handfuls of the stuff. I told him all it took was a little dip in the shorts. Otherwise, the guys would be aware that there was something foreign in their underwear. In that case, the they will just not put the clothing on, and the trick fails to reach its payoff.

Steve Kerr and Jud Buechler may be smiling here, but Dennis Rodman's Ben-Gay trick left them hot. (Photo courtesy of Bill Wennington)

But in Washington, Dennis was subtle, and Steve and Jud put their clothes on after the game. They didn't say anything right away. We got on the airplane and still we got nothing out of them. Dennis started cussing at me, telling me we should have put more on. I told him to relax, he would get his satisfaction.

Steve told me later that it was very hot, and that both he and Jud knew they had been had. But they didn't want to give us the satisfaction of knowing we had scored practical joke points on them.

Appreciating Regularity

Ask anyone who is a parent of a school-age kid, and they can tell you what is wrong with professional sports today. There might be a variety of answers, but one thing that will be mentioned for sure is that kids can't develop a relationship with their favorite team's roster because the rosters change so much year after year, even on the good teams. Free agency is a great thing for the players, but it is a hindrance to cohesiveness and consistency on any professional sports roster these days.

But the Chicago Bulls, through all of their championships, maintained a roster of the same 10 guys year after year, and I think that went a long way in helping us be so successful. Remember the first three-peat team? It was Michael Jordan, Scottie Pippen, Horace Grant, Bill Cartwright and John Paxson in the starting lineup. The second team was Stacey King, B.J. Armstrong, Will Perdue, Craig Hodges and Scott Williams.

For the second three-peat, the starters were Michael Jordan, Scottie Pippen, Dennis Rodman, Luc Longley and Ron Harper. The bench was Toni Kukoc, Bill Wennington, Steve Kerr, Jud Buechler and Randy Brown. We always had that third center—James Edwards, Robert Parish or Joe Kleine—and then there were the others, like Dickey Simpkins or Jason Caffey, Rusty LaRue and Scott Burrell.

But having 10 guys for fans to latch onto, guys you knew from previous seasons, that had to be a huge part of our basketball success and our off-the-court popularity. There were T-shirts produced with the 10 of us on them. It was clear who the Bulls were, up and down the roster.

Even when we added players, it seemed we picked up guys who fit in with what we already had. They weren't guys who were going to demand a lot of attention, or make waves, or go off on their own. They were guys who mixed well with us, and even managed to add to the chemistry of the team.

It was good we didn't have to make any big adjustments, because our summers were so short, with the previous season lasting so long, we wouldn't have had a lot of time to get to know each other.

Bad Habits

We didn't win games using luck. We didn't need luck, because we had Michael and Scottie and Dennis.

But we did have guys who had routines for getting ready for a game, routines that didn't waver. Call them superstitions if you wish, but they were part of the daily routine.

Michael had to wear his Carolina blue shorts under his Bulls shorts. I think Michael's dedication to maintaining a relationship with his college extended far beyond that of most guys in the league.

Scottie Pippen was the caffeine guy, coffee usually. It was a cup of coffee an hour before the game. In some of the places we went, I can't imagine it was good coffee, either. He also took ginseng, which had a quick run through the NBA there for awhile. I didn't get it.

Dennis took a shower before the game. Even when he didn't show up until late, well after the scheduled time for players to arrive at the arena, he would jump into the shower right before the team meeting. He would show up wet in the locker room for our pregame talk to go over our game plan.

I didn't have any real pregame habits. I did say a little prayer for my family and my team, to make sure everyone stayed healthy, before every game.

There were guys who wanted to shoot before a game, and guys who wouldn't do it no matter what. Luc, Steve, Jud and Randy all liked to go out and get loose. Toni would do it once in a while. Michael and Scottie stopped doing it, and Dennis was rarely there in time to shoot before the game.

The Top Jerry

The Bulls are owned by a group of investors headed by Jerry Reinsdorf, who also owns the Chicago White Sox.

As an owner, Jerry was far more knowledgeable about baseball than basketball, and he pretty much kept his distance from our team. He was the front man, and he was responsible for most of the business decisions, but we players didn't have much to do with him. He was far more visible at White Sox games, and I actually saw him at Comiskey Park as much as I did at the United Center.

We would see Jerry at Bulls games during the playoffs. That was about the only time he was front and center. He was there to get the trophy at the championship games, and he was very supportive of all of us. He rarely said much to the media, and when he did, it was respectful of us as individuals, even if he didn't like the players' union or the amounts of money the superstars were making.

Jerry lives in Phoenix during the winter, and we would see him when we got down there for our annual game against the Suns.

All Wet

After we won the first championship, the team got into a water fight in the postgame locker room. Champagne was sticky, and a lot of guys wanted to drink it and not waste it. Water was easier to throw. We had buckets of it, and everyone was getting nailed.

Mr. Reinsdorf was in the equipment room at the United Center after the game, and he was having a cigar-smoking party with some of the team management. I went in, said hello, thanked him for making me a part of the team, and drenched him with a full bucket of water.

Sometimes we celebrated with champagne, but more often we had water fights and drank the champagne. (Photo courtesy of Bill Wennington)

He laughed, and seemed to think it was funny, but he wasn't pleased that I put out the cigar he had just lit.

I'm pretty sure Mr. Reinsdorf knew everything that was going on with the team, but he seemed to do a good job of hiring people he could trust to do their jobs. Then he lets them do it.

That's probably the best kind of owner to have.

Jerry Reinsdorf was always fully supportive of his general manager, Jerry Krause. No man took as much grief as Krause did, in the Chicago media and with the fans. We were winning championships, and the man who put the team together couldn't catch a break. But Mr. Reinsdorf had Jerry Krause's back. I think that kind of loyalty doesn't exist much in sports anymore, either.

We Will Always Have Paris

There were many rewards for winning NBA titles. There were rings, and hats, and T-shirts, and playoff money, and free meals around town. But after we won in 1997, we got a special prize.

We got to go to Paris.

In the late 1980s, the NBA got involved in something called the McDonald's Championship. It was a tournament sponsored by FIBA, the international governing body for basketball. The idea was to try to create an international basketball competition that would involve the NBA champion every other year, sort of an attempt to make a club championship similar to the ones they have in soccer.

It started in 1987 with the Milwaukee Bucks, who hosted several foreign teams in Milwaukee for a series of games. For a number of years, it was an annual affair, with the Boston Celtics, Denver Nuggets, New York Knicks and Los Angeles Lakers representing the league.

The Phoenix Suns went to Europe in 1993, then in 1995 the tournament requested the NBA champion from the previous season attend the tournament. So the Houston Rockets went in 1995, and in 1997 it was our turn.

The NBA got involved because it was so intent on making inroads into the European market for merchandise sales. As the Olympics indicated, the popularity of basketball was exploding around the world, and teams everywhere were getting better. The Yugoslavian team, which became the Croatian and Serbian teams, was developing into a world-class talent, and the club basketball in Greece, Spain and Italy was very popular.

That was also about the time there was talk of a European NBA division, which was fun to think about. Imagine the road trip to play franchises in London, Barcelona, Paris and Munich. Free agents would flock to those teams for a quick, paid European vacation.

Going to Paris in October to play basketball was not the dream assignment you might think it would be. For one thing, we had to start our training camp early so that we were in some kind of shape for the games, which were played in the middle of October. We were already suffering our second short summer because of the length of the playoffs, and then the NBA threw in a couple of games in Paris, which of course required overseas flights. Nobody wanted to go, and the organization was displeased about the required extra basketball.

As nice as it sounds to go to Paris, it tossed a monkey wrench into all of our summer plans and took away a couple of weeks of rest and relaxation.

Everyone brought their families, except for me. My son Robbie's birthday was during that trip, and he would have had to miss a week of school. The combination made Anne and me decide it would be better for Robbie to stay at home. Robbie had already been to Italy.

Most everyone had some family member there, though. For the families, it was a nice trip.

We all had a good time. There were some breaks in the practice and game schedule so we could walk around the city and do some sightseeing. Paris is like all the other beautiful metropolitan cities of the world: you have to walk it to appreciate it.

It was, however, still training camp time, and we had two games to play. Not only that; they were games we could not lose. The NBA had not lost a game in international competition, and we could not be the first.

We had practice every day, including the day we arrived after our eight-hour flight.

Getting There

We flew to Paris on a really tricked-out 747, so our ride over was very comfortable. There was an upstairs area that nobody went up to initially. I got up there and it was like a big bedroom. So I went up there to lay down. Then some other guys showed up and it became the card lounge, until broadcaster Neil Funk found out about it and turned it into a smoking lounge.

We flew all night, and when we landed, it was actually the middle of the afternoon in Paris. So we went straight to practice in an attempt to get acclimated to the change in time quicker. Phil actually worked us pretty hard, hoping we would go get some sleep right away and get onto a regular body-clock schedule.

The games weren't difficult, even though the European teams played hard against us. What was weird was that the players from the other team were asking Michael and Scottie and Dennis for autographs before and after the game. The fans were really excited. Everyone liked to compare us to the Beatles, and maybe this trip was something like when the Beatles came to the United States the first time.

For us, it was all business. We had two games and left. It was a whirlwind visit.

We played a team from France called PSG Racing, and that game was closer than expected, 89-82. Then we played Olympiakos Pireo of Greece in the second game and won that going away 104-78. What was most interesting about that game was that we played against a center named Dragan Tarlac, whom the Bulls had drafted in 1995. Everyone wanted to get a look at him, to see if he would come over and be talented as Toni Kukoc was when he finally came to the States.

Tarlac eventually came to the Bulls in 2000, played all of 43 games and left.

There were also teams from Italy and Spain in the tournament.

Las Vegas

In October of 1997, after our second championship, we had a preseason game in Las Vegas. We had a game in California a day before that, then went to Las Vegas. I'm not sure how that happened, because there was a lot of controversy surrounding Las Vegas as an expansion city for professional sports teams. Plus, we had Dennis, who lived for Las Vegas. The potential for trouble seemed quite clear. I'm not sure what the thinking was there.

I remember we played the Seattle SuperSonics in that game, because I got to see Detlef Schrempf, who was my teammate when we were with Dallas.

We had a night in between games, and Phil let us go to Las Vegas early, so we had a night to play Vegas games before we played the basketball game. Then Phil decided to let us stay the night in Las Vegas after the game rather than fly out. It had to be a reward for the two previous championships, and a way to mentally relax before the start of what we knew was going to be our toughest season.

I have played preseason games on Indian reservations, in small towns through the midwest. We had a game in Peoria, Illinois, and we went to North or South Dakota once, I remember. The preseason was a time to take our show on the road to places that would never see an NBA franchise. Those games aren't bad, necessarily, but all we ever really did was pack up, get into town, try to find something to eat, play a game and leave. There was no identity to those games, unless you happened to be from that area.

The Las Vegas game was much more relaxing. It was near the end of training camp, kind of like a final blowout before we got serious again. It was a nice arrangement.

I could describe some of the things that went on that night (that I heard about, actually) but what happens in Vegas stays in Vegas.

God's Country

We had a preseason game in Chapel Hill, North Carolina, one year, a big return to God's country for Michael. He talked about that all the time, being from God's country. When Charlotte entered the league, we had to hear about it. Blue sky stuff.

Talk about your home game away from home! Michael had so many fans at those Charlotte games, you would have thought we were at the United Center rather than the Charlotte Coliseum.

Scottie Asks Out

The 1997-98 season was our most difficult. We were tired, and we knew it was our last season together. We had a target, to match the Bulls from earlier in the decade and win a three-peat. But the grind of the two previous seasons and all the psychological effects of the team's internal battles was going to wear on us.

Besides that, Scottie Pippen was injured from the start of the season, and we missed him on the floor.

Scottie was at practice every day, and was still a significant member of the team. But he was frustrated by his physical condition and by the fact that once again he had been the subject of trade talk in the summer. The Bulls were thinking about breaking us up before we were ready to see it all end, and Scottie was the target of most of the rumors in league circles. He was the most valuable member of the team besides Michael, and the Bulls could not get caught talking about trading Michael. There was talk of him going to Boston, I think for Antoine Walker, and Scottie considered it disrespectful. He wanted to be one of those players who played his entire career with one team, and he was getting to realize that might not happen for him.

We went on the West Coast trip in November of that year, and Scottie went with us. While in Los Angeles, he made big news by saying he was never going to play for the Bulls again. He said when he got well, he was going to ask for a trade. For three days on the trip, that was the talk, that Scottie wanted out.

We all talked about it, but we knew it was more a frustration thing. We also knew that the Bulls weren't going to make any trades in the middle of the season that had already been called "The Last Dance". Scottie was under contract, and that was it. When he got well, he played for us, and his demand was forgotten.

Illusions

Dennis was making enough money, and had enough contacts in the city, that he managed to become "owner" of a bar in downtown Chicago. It was called Illusions, on Ontario, right in the middle of party central.

There wasn't a nightclub in Chicago Dennis hadn't already visited. I think he wanted to have a place he considered his own, even though he made himself at home everywhere he went. The club scene in Chicago was really going strong when Dennis was in town.

I went to the grand opening of Illusions, as did about half the team. I remember that Jerry Krause and Phil Jackson both showed up. We all popped in, got our free drinks, congratulated Dennis and left. I also remember that the grand opening took place on a school night, which might not have been the best time, not that Dennis would have understood that as a consideration. Dennis didn't have school nights.

It was a fun experience and a decent bar, and as soon as Dennis left town after the 1998 season, the bar closed down.

Tough Talk

The start of the 1997-98 season had that kind of pale air about it, because there had been so much talk of it being our last season together. So Phil made a public statement that he was going to make this a fun season for everyone, and that he was going to do whatever he could to make it enjoyable for the players.

Privately, in our first meeting that season, he told us, "I want you guys to stop and smell the roses, and enjoy the season as it is happening around you. I want you to see what is going on around us." It was Phil acting the role of parent, telling us to appreciate the good life we were leading.

Phil was very good at trying to make us see some kind of meaning to what we were doing beyond scoring more points than the opposition.

I remember the one time we did something out of the ordinary was in New York, when we got on a bus to go to practice for a game against the Knicks. Instead of heading to our practice facility, we ended up going to the port to take a ride on the Staten Island ferry. That was our practice that day, to go on the ferry, go to the other side, come back and then spend the day enjoying New York.

There were many occasions when we would gather in the lobby of our hotel to go to practice and Phil would come down and announce "no practice today." Or we would be on a plane heading somewhere, and he would announce no practice once we landed. He wanted us to relax. He realized we were an older group, we already knew what we had to do, and he trusted us to be prepared mentally and physically to do it.

He took care of us. I think he was very conscious of that the last year.

Hoping and Hopeless

All through our championship run, at the end of each season, there was talk and concern about when Phil would leave because of his poor working relationship with Jerry Krause, or whether the Bulls would actually trade Scottie, or how long Michael was going to play. Going through the 1997-98 season, even with the preseason pronouncement from Phil that this was the last season, there was this little hope that something would happen and we would come back for one more season.

But I think we all knew we were done.

We won that last championship in Utah, and even as we were celebrating, and I was spraying Dennis's girlfriend, Carmen Elektra, with champagne, you could see the reactions in the eyes of the people around you. You could see that everyone knew it was all over, the party was finally done.

We were excited to have won again, but there was a sense of finality just minutes after the final buzzer had gone off.

Maybe I was reading into it, because the end was certainly on my mind. But I am sure there was not the same jubilation and excitement that we had before. You could see there was something else in the air.

Double Team

During one summer, Dennis had time to make a movie. It was called *Double Team* (a basketball reference, even though it wasn't a basketball film) and it starred Jean-

Claude Van Damme, which should give you some idea what kind of movie it was.

Dennis was thinking about what he was going to do when his basketball career was over, and he realized the entertainment industry might have a place for him. He had tried some professional wrestling, which seemed like a natural venue, and he was also thinking an acting career might be plausible. It was a little odd, because Dennis really was a shy guy, but he had a presence that transferred to the big screen.

There was a premiere opening in Los Angeles for the movie when we were out there for a game. Actually, it was more of a private showing, a screening to let Dennis see how he liked it. So Dennis invited the team, and I remember I got to meet the wrestler Hulk Hogan, who had become friendly with Dennis.

The movie was all right. Dennis did mumble a bit, but that was the way he spoke with us. I understood him because I was accustomed to his way of speaking.

It was a fun way to spend an evening, but I knew I didn't have to get my tux pressed to attend any parties celebrating Dennis's Academy Award victory.

Old Shoe

The last time we went to New York, Michael made a splash by wearing his old Air Jordans, the red and black ones, the ones that started the shoe craze for Michael. Maybe he was planning to market them as retro apparel, I don't know. I do know they were hurting his feet. They were 15 years old, and shoes had improved a lot over that time. But he played in them, and everyone got a story out of that.

Trampoline Hands

Michael called me "Trampoline Hands" because when I got in the game, I would shoot right away, as soon as I touched the ball. The way I saw it, that is why they put me in the game, to shoot. Phil would call a play where I would get the ball, and he always told me, "We need you to shoot the ball." So I said, "All right," and I never looked back.

It was Phil's philosophy that if a play is called for you and you don't shoot the ball when you have it, then you are messing up the play. Everyone is in position to react to your shot, and if you pass up an open shot, our offense has broken down.

Michael used to kid me that throwing the ball to me was just like redirecting it toward the basket, like throwing it off a trampoline.

Of course, Michael was never shy about shooting, but that apparently, is another matter all together.

Phil and Jerry

Phil Jackson was this tall, handsome, intellectual, erudite basketball coach. Jerry Krause was this short, stocky, single-minded general manager. They had nothing in common, and eventually they had no relationship at all.

But as a player, the only fair thing to do was find a way to co-exist with both of them. They were both there, and around. As a player, you had to do what the coach said, and the coach did make Jerry a focal point of our motivation at times. But as a person, you tried to understand everybody. You wanted to make your life mesh in all aspects.

It was hard to maintain a balance in your life when things were so skewed with the Phil and Jerry situation.

At the end of the 1998 season, it was hard to keep your mind focused on basketball. We had our team problems, knowing that Phil was getting ready to leave, and his relationship with Jerry was deteriorating daily. At the same time, the lockout of players was about to get underway, as league management and the players' union argued over a new collective bargaining agreement, and those of us who were going to play the next season had to worry about that.

But I think Phil liked the distractions because they took our minds off of basketball. He wanted us to be hitting on all cylinders when we got to the playoffs, and he figured we would be better off if we waited a while before we focused completely on basketball.

Phil liked to talk about the distractions, and we players did, too. One topic that we players discussed regularly was the atmosphere at the Berto Center, our practice facility.

Things were getting tense. You could see it in the eyes of the secretaries. Nobody knew what was going to happen from day to day. Jerry and Phil each had offices upstairs, about 10 yards apart, and you didn't know what would happen if and when they passed each other in the hallways up there.

I guess it is part of the story of our championships, and we all survived it. But it would have been nice if there had not been that undercurrent of negative emotion. Who knows? Without it, we might have gone on to win a few more championships.

CHAPTER ELEVEN

Phil's Plan

Motivation was always a problem for professional basketball players. All of the good teams made the playoffs, the bad teams didn't, the season was long, the travel was tedious, and the games sometimes took on a feeling of sameness.

We were getting paid lots of money, most players had guaranteed contracts, and Friday often turned into Saturday without us really being aware of it.

Phil Jackson was very adept at keeping everyone motivated to play to the best of their ability. That included the bench players, the ones who played little and the ones who sometimes played not at all.

It was hard to complain about your role on a team that won all the time. When you were on the Bulls in the 1990s, you couldn't go to the media and say, "If I was playing more, we would be winning more." We won all the time. Complaining about your playing time when you are on a championship team seemed like a childish thing to do.

But there were players who wanted to vent about not being in the daily rotation. Although Phil did a nice job of using his bench, at least until the playoffs came around, there were still some players who had issues about how they were being used.

But just when a player was about to explode because he was not playing enough, Phil somehow sensed that and would come over and pat him on the back and reel him back in to the team picture. He was a great coach at reading body language and stress. He seemed to have the knack of knowing when to come to you just as you were about to lose it at a practice or a game or a team meeting. He would not only tell you that you were needed for the next game, he would make sure to use you, and make you a part of the process once again.

Practice Games

Phil ran our practices like he ran our games. Our substitution patterns in practice were similar to our substitution patterns in games.

When we ran offenses or defenses, Steve Kerr and I would be on the sideline, which is where we were when games started. Phil trained our bodies and minds to be prepared to come in and play on a regular rotation, after the game had been going on for several minutes. I thought that was very smart. I was on other teams where you had the starters practice against the bench guys at all times, and then game days were entirely different than practice days.

In games, the bench players seldom played as a unit of five. Instead, we would go in two at a time and spell starters, who would then come back in with another couple of reserves. It was important for me to know how to play with Michael Jordan, or for Ron Harper to know how to play with Randy Brown as his backcourt mate. Phil knew that, and he ran practices with two separate teams, each with some starters and some bench players.

Playing for Fun

I don't know if Phil started this system, but he would regularly give the starters, or anyone who played 30 minutes the night before, the day off from practice the next day. The subs, anybody who didn't play 30 minutes the night before, would have to practice, but they were usually fun workouts, obviously different from the practices we ran with the starters around.

We would play shooting games, or drills contests. Sometimes we even just had foot races. But Phil made us work as teams in most of the contests. He would pick captains, and we would select teams. He used those selections as motivation as well, sometimes giving the captain's job to players who needed a boost.

Bigs Vs. Littles

We were always out of town on Thanksgiving because of the United Center schedule, and we always had a practice on Thanksgiving Day. It was the annual Bigs against

Littles game, and it turned out to be more than just a fun day of practice and a little aerobic exercise. It became a traditional battle of centers and forwards against guards and swing players.

In fact, it was in my first year with the Bulls, 1993, that Will Perdue got his thumb   broken in the Bigs vs. Littles game. That gave me my chance to play more, and helped me gain some of Phil's confidence.

Good game, that Bigs vs. Littles thing.

Playing big guys on one team and little guys on another gave both sides a chance to pretend they were something else. It gave the big guys a chance to play point guard, run the offense, act like Magic Johnson. It gave the guards a chance to post up their big teammates, dribble in the post, acting like Shaquille O'Neal or Patrick Ewing or somebody like that.

Once the games got going, the guards would try to run us big guys into the ground. They would play up and down, while the bigs would play more of a patterned offense.

Phil would make sure both teams ran our offense as much as possible. Again, it was a learning tool. It gave the Littles a chance to see the responsibilities of the big men in the triangle offense, and it gave the Bigs a chance to see the different choices the guards had to make in setting us up offensively. We got to find out how guards identified the cutters and where the passes would be coming from.

The point guard for the big guys was always Toni Kukoc, although we all got to bring the ball up once or twice, dribble between our legs, that sort of thing.

The littles liked to practice their spin moves in the post, and they liked to run around setting up passing opportunities out of the post.

Where Did Scottie Play?

There were two variables in the Bigs vs. Littles Thanksgiving games. One was Scottie Pippen, who could be claimed by either side. The other variable was Michael Jordan, who didn't often play.

Scottie was the swing guy. Since Toni Kukoc usually played with the Bigs, Scottie was given to the Littles, especially if we had a full roster of healthy players. There were times when he would end up with the Bigs, who were at a disadvantage in the games from a scoring standpoint, but he was mostly with the Littles.

Phil usually let Michael sit out the game. Michael was still a 40-minute guy, and always in incredible shape, and since the game was just a way to get some activity over the holiday weekend, Michael wasn't required to play.

Unfortunately, that usually meant Michael was wearing the whistle, and he was a horrible referee. If you ever thought an NBA ref had an agenda, you had to think Michael went to that job with a laundry list of schemes.

Sometimes he would just decide which team was going to win and his calls would go that way. It was all in fun, and we had a good time with it, but you know if Michael was in the game and not getting the calls he thought he deserved, he would have been most unhappy.

Here is how the games would go: a big man, usually Toni but occasionally someone else, would bring the ball up. The guards would pressure the big man and force him into a turnover, run down the court past us and score. If it got out of hand in favor of the Littles, that is when Phil would give us Scottie for point guard services.

Of course, the Bigs could always post up the Littles if we got the ball past midcourt. That's when the Littles would do anything they could think of to stop the shot. The would double-team the post, start cherry picking from the other side. Basically, they cheated.

Let's face it; the Littles were better shooters, in most cases, and quicker. The Bigs weren't built for competition against guards. That's why Toni Kukoc was such a huge commodity for the Bigs.

I do recall the Bigs won the game once in my years with the Bulls.

Before the Game

For 7:30 games at the United Center, we were required to show up by 6 p.m. That was also the time the media was allowed into our locker room for pregame conversations and injury updates.

Dennis wasn't usually in the locker room by 6 p.m., but he got close a few times.

At 6:45, the locker room doors would close, and we would begin our pregame preparation in earnest. We had a pregame strategy meeting with Phil, who would tell us what we needed to do in that specific game. Every now and then, he would actually poll the team or ask our opinions about what would work or not work. We had already gone over much of our game plan in shootaround that day, but Phil wanted to remind us, just in case we had forgotten between lunch and dinner.

When we got on the court, we were all business. (AP/WWP)

The assistant coach who studied that team would give the scouting report, going over the short list of details we needed.

It was a dead serous time, get down and focus time. It was Phil's way of getting us into game mode. Nothing else matters now.

This was our final gathering as a team. Phil used to tell us to get serious the moment we arrived at the arena, but the real business started at about five minutes to 7 p.m., when the team gathered together.

We even watched some film in these meetings, even though we had done that in the shootaround in the morning. Phil wasn't going to let any details escape us, assuming we were listening. The advantage of having a veteran team is that most of us did listen.

What Time Is it?

At about 7:15, we would come out of the locker room where we were going over strategy, and walk out into the hallway of the backstage area of the United Center. We shared the building with the Chicago Blackhawks, and our locker room was down the hall from theirs.

We always wanted to run out onto the floor as a team, so we would gather ourselves just beyond the entranceway to the actual basketball floor. We always had to wait for someone (it was usually Dennis), so we would all go through our routines, tying our laces one last time, putting on our snap-button sweats (which we were required to wear), and stretching.

Once everybody was there, we would get in a huddle, and Michael would say something about what we were about to do. He did a nice job of being game-specific, rather than saying the same thing all the time.

Then another player would yell out, "What time is it?" and we would all shout out, "Game time," with a kind of bark at the end. That signified we were ready to do battle. It was just a way of having a routine to collectively pull everybody in to fight for a common cause and have a common goal.

The "What time is it?" job fell to Ron Harper most of the time through our championship seasons. He did it once, and everybody liked the way he did it. I remember Steve Kerr used to do it before Michael returned in 1995. A couple of other guys got a chance. I know Jud did it once or twice, and I think Randy Brown had the job, too.

Yes, Ron would stutter at times when he did it, but I think that made it more effective. And it gave us something to kid him about.

We would wait for Dennis a lot. He just liked to take his time about things. It was not that he was late, he was just the last one there most of the time. It wasn't like a five-minute wait for 11 guys. The time between the first person and the final person may have been all of a couple of minutes.

We ran out onto the floor in a particular order, but I don't remember the order now. I don't think it was anything anybody decided on, it just happened. When the season started, the first time we went out, you got into a spot, and that was your spot.

I know Ron Harper went first. I think Jud Buechler was in front of me, or Michael. I think Dennis and Luc came out last all the time. We were creatures of habit, and it really made us focus a bit more.

When someone went on the injured list, of course, the order changed. And I don't recall it ever being an issue with anyone, about who was going on the floor first or last.

Introductions

The Bulls were among the first teams to have the really insanely elaborate introductions. We had the lights out, the spot lights sweeping over the floor, the laser show going on. We had the film short showing on the big screen above the floor. It took a very long time to get our games going because of the introductions.

I know that the Bulls started this routine, but some teams eventually got carried away with it. And it was usually teams that didn't have any championships or success to crow about. It was always a little weird to see teams go through these elaborate pregame shows when their teams had not had a winning season in years.

Eventually, teams started with the indoor fireworks, and we got tired of that. In fact, it got to the point where so many fireworks were going off, some games would start out in kind of a haze.

We had the song, the Gary Glitter "Rock and Roll" song, that we were introduced by. I know I still get chills every time I hear that song.

But the truth is, players don't like the long introductions. You get yourself ready to play, then you have to sit back and watch 10 minutes of pomp and circumstance, and all for a regular-season game, one of 82. It would be different if it were just for the playoffs, I guess, but it wasn't.

Of course, when Toronto and Vancouver came into the league, we would have to do both national anthems when the Raptors or Grizzlies were involved.

It was our rule, and maybe even a league rule, that we had to stand on the foul line extended, facing the American flag. In that instance, guys would usually go to the same spot. I liked to stand at the elbow of the key.

Hearing Voices

Randy Brown was a pretty good singer, the best on the team. He had a high voice. He liked to sing in different voices. He was very entertaining. He was just a very funny man, and he had a lot of entertaining talents.

He liked to sing songs from television commercials, or things you would hear on the radio. He wouldn't sing seriously, it was more in jest. But he probably could have sung seriously if he wanted to.

Uniforms

In 1997, the NBA decided to try to make a little more money off the Bulls, and they gave us black uniforms to use as a third, alternate jersey color. It was an obvious marketing gimmick, and it shouldn't have mattered to us at all. Except that the first two times we wore the dumb things, we lost. We were a superstitious bunch, and it certainly seemed like the uniforms were making us lose. So, the next time they got dragged out, we were all over our equipment man, John Ligmanowski, asking him why we had to wear them again.

Michael was without question the most superstitious of us all. He hated the black uniforms initially because he believed they were bad luck. But the league mandated that we wear them a certain number of times during the season, so we decided that if we had to wear them, we were going to get the games over quickly. You would have to go back and look, but we were extra determined in those games to get the outcome decided in a hurry.

Black Shoes

Back in 1989, I believe, former Bulls forward Brad Sellers started a trend that really took off. He probably wishes he could have made some money off of it. Brad talked the Bulls into wearing black socks for the playoffs. It was about that time the Bulls started winning playoff series, and two years later they won the league title for the first time. It was all in the socks.

After awhile, other teams started wearing black socks for the playoffs, too. Imitation being the highest form of flattery, and all that.

At one point, somebody on our team suggested we wear black socks all the time, in the regular season, too. That was nixed right away. Just for the playoffs.

The fact of the matter was, it was not a good look. The white guys understood that we just looked really silly that way. It made us look slow, which makes sense since we were, at least by comparison.

But everyone went along, because that is what the Bulls had done for years. After about the second game, you get accustomed to the look. But I will tell you that the first time you put on black socks to play basketball, the contrast is startling.

If anybody complained that the look was just bad, someone would offer the reminder that a lot of guys too cool to wear black socks with basketball shoes were sitting at home, about to watch us on TV.

Fashion

We had no fashion police on the team, but we really didn't need any. Everyone looked pretty decent most of the time.

Michael, of course, always wanted to look good. He had an image to project, and he did so, no matter where we were or what we were doing. He was always dressed properly. Scottie Pippen was the same way. Scottie wore a different style than Michael, but they were always groomed.

Dennis was a different story. You would look at him and say he didn't care about the way he looked, but he really did. He was just at the opposite end of the looking-good spectrum. He wanted to project an image that he didn't care what he looked like, but he put a lot of effort into wearing clothes that weren't coordinated properly. His appearance was so random that you just knew a lot of thought went into it. It couldn't be that inconsistent all the time. It had to be planned.

Randy Brown was always well dressed and finely manicured. Toni was up and down, but when he made the effort, he would come in looking good. He liked to get dressed up and go out. He cleaned up pretty well.

Luc Longley was the one who truly didn't worry too much about how he looked. He wore Australian casual, whatever that was. He always had interesting footwear. I wasn't much of a fashion guy. I tried to look neat and clean, had my shirt tucked in.

We didn't really have any slobs, except Dennis, who was slob chic.

Ron Harper tried to keep up with Michael in appearance, just as he tried to do in basketball terms. Ron kind of jumped on board the ship Michael built. Ron always showed up with the same level of attire as Michael. They were both extremely fashionable.

CHAPTER TWELVE

Nicknames

We all take pride in the nicknames of the teams we play on, even if they are silly or weird or have double meanings. I was a King, and a Maverick, and then a Bull. By the time I got to Chicago, the team nickname had become synonymous with success, and the logo was everywhere in town. There was a certain amount of pride to wearing our sweats and our uniforms and our practice gear with the logo on it.

By the time the league got around to expanding in the late 1980s, it seemed like maybe they were running out of good team names. It wasn't until Miami and Orlando came along that the league went to the singular nickname—the Miami Heat, the Orlando Magic. The Minnesota Timberwolves was a good name, with a great logo. What they were thinking in Toronto with the Raptors I will never know.

What's kind of weird about being associated with the Bulls beyond my playing days is that the players on the team no longer associate the logo or team name with success. It doesn't mean anything special for them to be a Bull. They could just as easily, and with the same significance, be a Pacer or a Piston or a Buck. I guess that is just part of the historical position of what has been, what is and what will be.

It is difficult to be where I was, and the pride we had in protecting our image, the image we had of ourselves, and to see how it is being treated now. It is certainly different, whether it is good or bad. It is no longer the same. It has taken six years, but the championship feeling has worn off. The quality of the play is not the same, the records are obviously different, and it all hurts to watch.

For the Bulls in 2004, they are at an opposite end of the scale from where we were at in the mid- to late 1990s.

Mascots

If nicknames were hard to get accustomed to, or hard to define, mascots were completely out of control. Things got so unusual with mascots that we ended up needing two of them.

We always had Benny the Bull. In fact, the man inside Benny the Bull, Dan LeMonnier, just retired. Benny the Bull was the kid's mascot, very safe, happy, bouncy. He didn't do much in terms of an actual act, but he always managed to make the kids in the arena smile.

I always liked Benny, and when you understand what he is there for, you have to appreciate the fact he makes it work.

Now, there were many Benny-like mascots in the league. The Philadelphia 76ers had the Philly Phanatic, who was just as big, in size, as Benny, but was really funny, too. He had a good act.

Burnie, I think, was the name of the Miami Heat flame-head mascot, and he was also very active, with lots of funny bits.

But at some point, teams adopted a more muscular, high-flying kind of mascot. The Gorilla in Phoenix was able to cross over from being a funny, goofy mascot to being the acrobatic type. The Charlotte Hornets came up with Hugo, and he was nothing but a slam-dunk artist, but a really good one.

When those acrobatic mascots became the big thing in the league, we players really got into it. It was something new, and these guys were clearly athletic, and we liked their shows as much as we enjoyed the kiddy kind of entertainment.

We understood Benny the Bull was a part of the kid show, and we knew, because of the size of the costume, that Benny was never going to be making any slam dunks, even off of trampolines.

So then the Bulls got their own acrobat. He was a meaner and leaner Bull, and he was called Da Bull, after the *Saturday Night Live* skit about Chicago sports fans that deemed the team Da Bulls, and the football team Da Bears, and Mike Ditka Da Coach.

Da Bull was indeed more acrobatic and athletic. He had one problem. He missed a lot of dunks. I mean, he missed a LOT of dunks. The big joke around the team was that Michael once sat down with the guy who was Da Bull and told him, "Don't you ever let anyone know who is in there. If people find out you are a brother, it is going to look bad for everybody."

We were excited to have a mascot with his kind of ability. We were no longer second fiddle to Charlotte, and we actually had the bonus of having two identifiable mascots. Everybody was open to the addition of Da Bull, until he started missing dunks.

The good news is, he got better.

The Spinners

There are lots of reasons for coaches to call timeout. There are strategy timeouts, there are rest timeouts, there are timeouts to stop the other team from having long rallies. There are TV timeouts, there are injury timeouts.

But somewhere along the line timeouts became money makers for the teams. If a team could present any kind of "entertainment" during the timeout, and that entertainment could be sponsored, teams would present it without hesitation or embarrassment.

It was a way for the fans to pass the time and for teams to make some extra dough. For players, it was at first entertaining, then a nuisance, and then something to ignore.

If you were in the game, or about to go in the game, you had to ignore what was going on around you and pay attention to the coach. But if you were not about to enter the game, it was hard not to notice that doughnuts were racing each other on the big board, or small infants were crawling to their parents in a diaper derby, or somebody was taking a half-court shot for $10,000.

We had the donut race, a very popular feature. Three donuts would be pictured racing each other around the big screen three times, with a winner declared at the end. Fans would receive cards with donut names on them, and if your donut won, you could redeem the card for a free donut.

When they announced those kinds of events, the announcer would say, "No wagering, please" but he never got the message to Michael, who always wanted to bet somebody on the outcome of the race.

He wanted to bet on the outcome because he already knew the outcome.

Michael would go to the engineers who run the big board before the game and find out which tape they were putting in, and which donut was going to win that night. Then, he would get ready for the donut race timeout by finding someone to wager, and wouldn't you know it, Michael would win every time.

I remember he got Scott Burrell, who was with us in 1997-98, several times before Scott caught on.

While we tried to ignore the contests, we did try to catch the spinning bat guys on a regular basis. This was a contest where two men from the crowd would spin their head upon the end of a bat 10 times, then attempt to make a basket. They were almost always too dizzy to do much for several seconds, and the really gung-ho guys usually fell down, which always brought a laugh. We loved the guys who crashed into things, too, like the basket standard or the side seats.

We also kept our eyes on any moment when a fan from the stands stood to make a ton of money with one half-court or three-quarter-court shot. We saw some people win, but not often. We just made sure not to miss those moments.

Phil the Genius

Everything surrounding a basketball game was an opportunity for Phil to gain an edge. He used the timeout entertainment to his advantage, which is another example of the man's intelligence and thoughtfulness.

Perhaps because he knew he couldn't keep us totally focused during a timeout when a couple of contestants are involved in a very loud karaoke contest a few feet away, Phil would spend the first minute of a timeout huddling with his assistant coaches, talking over strategy and what to say to the team. Then, when the timeout contest was winding down, he would stride over to the bench and give the team one quick instruction.

Phil was very cerebral in that sense. There have been studies done that say in the heat of a moment, you are not going to remember a lot of details. You are going to focus on one thing. So Phil would give us one play, one message, to take out to the court. Unless he was unhappy with our play, in which case he would rant. For the most part, we used timeouts to collect our thoughts. Phil probably did the same thing, collect himself to remember the game plan and avoid rash decisions.

Because Phil didn't talk the whole time during time-outs, we players had a chance to discuss the game, too. We would see things on the floor that needed to be addressed. Guys on the bench had a chance to talk to the starters and let them know what was going on out on the floor. It was a sign of the maturity of the team that we focused on the basketball process rather than nutty games being played around us.

Ugly Feet

We start running on hardwood floors in grade school, and we never stop. We get bigger and stronger, and maybe faster, and we keep running, on hardwood floors. Eventually, we start jumping (some of us, at least) and we land on hardwood floors. We stop fast, make sharp cuts, push the limits of our footwear, all on hardwood floors.

I've already told you how our knees feel at the end of a day. What I haven't told you yet is just how much abuse our feet suffer as a result of our chosen profession.

Basketball players have ugly feet. I'm about to tell you whose feet were the ugliest.

I remember one day when Randy Brown decided to hold court in the middle of the locker room, and his topic of the day was our toes. He described each of our feet, in detail, comparing them to different well-known disasters or ugly people. As I said, Randy was a funny guy, and he had a way of getting at us without offending us.

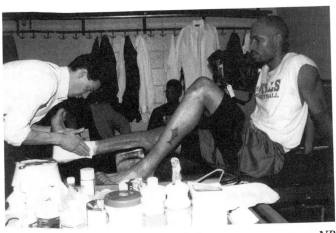

*Unless **absolutely** necessary, you don't want to get near an NBA player's **feet**. (Photo courtesy of Bill Wennington)*

Michael Jordan has god-awful looking feet. They are flat, probably from the impact of his jumps, and his toes are bent crooked, and they would all crunch up, like they were trying to achieve a fetal position.

Scottie's feet are not far behind. He has huge feet. I remember that Toni has long, skinny feet. Most of the rest of us seemed to fare pretty well in the foot department. I have a big bump on my right foot from breaking it in high school, but other than that, they are attractive enough.

The ugliest feet I've ever seen belonged to former Mavericks teammate James Donaldson. I don't even want to think about them. I might turn to stone.

The Brains

You would have to say Steve Kerr was the smartest of the bunch, at least in a book-smart sense. Michael was pretty smart, too, and he seemed to know a lot of about everything. He spent a lot of time in hotel rooms because he couldn't go out much; maybe he was boning up on CNN or the Discovery Channel.

We had a couple of guys who would do crossword puzzles, but I think they were just pretending to be smart. Actually, I remember Dennis doing crossword puzzles. Phil was big into crossword puzzles, too.

Money

Professional basketball players make a very good living, and as a result, we didn't talk about money much. We all had enough to get by, and were all very happy with what we had. If guys got into contract squabbles with the team, that was kept to themselves. It never entered our arena, and we didn't pry into numbers because it really wasn't our business. We each had our own contracts to worry about.

However, if someone bought a new car, that is where money came in. Everyone wanted to know how much the car cost. That was the first question, before we got to engine size, or accessories, or number of drink holders. Guys just wanted to know how much you paid for it.

There was one guy who would talk about contracts. Michael always wanted to know what you got if you signed a new deal. He wanted to bust you up. "I can't believe you are getting paid that much! Do they know what you do?"

Michael didn't mean anything by it. He didn't have to, he knew he was getting paid the most. He was just having fun, poking fun like everybody did about everything.

Professional basketball was a good living, whether you were at the high end or the low end.

Michael was at the high end, as he showed in his dress, his vehicles, his equipment. What was fun was to see rookies come into the league with big contracts and try to keep up with Michael. You would see guys paying their respects to Michael by buying the same kind of suit, a different suit for each day, and they didn't care that they were riding off their first contract while Michael was making $30 million a year. That was one time we laughed about spending habits. Other than that, it was just everybody enjoying the financial situation we were in.

Draft Picks

You know how the NBA draft works. The worst teams get the highest picks each year (unless they trade them away) and the better teams get the lower picks in each round. The NBA champion selects last in every round, unless it works out a trade.

So for the Bulls, as we were getting into our championship seasons, draft day was uneventful. We were going to get the 29th pick in the first round, and we usually didn't have room for him on our roster, anyway.

We didn't need anything on our roster. We had a good team and no 29th pick was going to make us much better.

In 1993, after the first three-peat was completed, we drafted Corie Blount, a forward out of Cincinnati. He was a very good athlete, and he was able to run up and down the floor well. But he found out that the NBA is a lot harder to get into, especially being drafted by such a good team. He was with the team, but he wasn't going to play much. Oddly enough, of course, it wasn't until 10 years later that he came back to the Bulls and became a contributor when the team was sliding downhill.

Corie did benefit from being drafted by the Bulls, however. He entered the league on a team that had strong discipline and work ethic. It gave him a good base to start from. I think a lot of guys come into the league, land on teams that aren't as good, don't have the same kind of discipline, a more lackadaisical attitude, and once you develop that kind of attitude, it is hard to break. If you start out that way and move to a team with a stronger coach, the adjustment is very difficult.

In 1994, we drafted Dickey Simpkins out of Providence, and he was on the roster for most of six seasons. But he got very little playing time, and he never got on Phil's good side. By the time he was done, he was bitter about his Bulls experience. The fact he was playing behind Dennis Rodman and Toni Kukoc for playing time hurt him tremendously.

In 1995, we got Jason Caffey, who was so much like Dickey Simpkins, they ended up getting traded for each other one time. Jason was with us for the three championship seasons.

That was the year Jerry Krause also picked Dragan Tarlac out of Greece, hoping he had found a Toni Kukoc in the post. He didn't join the team until 2000 and played about half a season.

In 1996, the Bulls drafted Travis Knight out of Connecticut and traded him right away. In 1997, we got Keith Booth out of Maryland, and he turned out to be an undersized forward.

Obviously, none of these guys had much to do with the championships the teams won from 1996 through 1998.

Although those three did not get a lot of playing time, Dickey came back to the Bulls after the titles were over and had some success as a veteran leader. I think Jason Caffey showed the most ability and potential, although he hated not playing. Dickey showed some ability at rebounding but didn't finish around the basket well. Corie was just a great athlete. When he went west, playing for the Lakers, I think, he found out his style was better suited to the west coast offense, a run-and-gun kind of game plan. That's how he managed to stay in the league as long as he did.

Treating Rookies

We didn't expect much from the rookies on the floor, other than hard work. But off the floor, rookies were ridden hard and put up wet.

It's pretty much the same throughout the league. Rookies had to bring donuts in for the team in the morning before practice. They had to carry bags from the bus to the plane, although that job got easier when we started chartering flights all the time.

Veterans would ask rookies to run their errands, pick up dry cleaning, return videos, that sort of thing. The worst thing a rookie could do in that situation was turn down a request. The more they resist, the more we veterans went at them with orders.

Corie Blount was funny about it. He complained, but he did so in a humorous way, and he always did the job. Jason Caffey got really frustrated by it, but he also did his job.

There was simply no way you could really resist. Turning us down would have been pure hell. Michael and Scottie would have been on top of you forever if you developed a reputation for avoiding your rookie duties.

It really wasn't that bad. A lot of it was inside the Berto Center; take something up to the secretary, get me a drink, pick up my bag, pack my shoes.

And for that, they got huge playoff bonus money.

Foreign Affair

From 1993 through 1998, the Bulls had a significant foreign influence. I am Canadian. Luc Longley was from Australia. Toni Kukoc was from Croatia. And we had Jud from California.

I think it made us a more interesting team. Although I had been in the United States my entire adult life, I still had some Canadian in me. Luc's accent, his "no worries" attitude, his lingo, all gave a unique down-under spice to the team. Toni's European influences were strong, in the way he played, and the way he was off the floor.

We got to know a little bit about each of them. Luc talked a lot about his life in Australia, about how beautiful the country was. He was buying a ranch back home, and he has getting a boat, and each year he talked about how much he was looking forward to relaxing on the beach. Of

International players like Luc Longley and Toni Kukoc fit in just fine in the family. (Photo courtesy of Bill Wennington)

course, for Luc, he spent the season in the American winter, and when he went home in our summer, it was winter in Australia. He looked forward to being able to enjoy an Australian summer.

Luc taught us all about Australian rules football, which was seen on TV occasionally. We even played it once, in the Berto Center, until the trainer came out and told us he didn't think it was a good idea. People get hurt in Australian rules football, even when they don't know what they are doing, exactly.

Luc gave John Ligmanowski an Australian rules football book one year after coming back from his home country. John still has it at the Berto Center.

Toni liked going home to Split, Croatia, which was near the beach as well. It was hard for Toni, because Croatia was in the midst of war when he first came over, and there was constant concern about family and friends.

Toni was extremely talented at soccer. He could handle a soccer ball as well as he handled a basketball, which was very good. He would entertain us before and after practice with his ball-handling skills. He liked to bounce the ball off his knee, bounce it off his head, drop it back down to his knee, then kick it up and into the basket. It was very entertaining, but not as entertaining as watching the rest of us try it.

I am Canadian, but Canada and the United States aren't that much different. About the only time I thought about being Canadian was when there was another Canadian around.

Competition

Michael Jordan had to retire from basketball three times before he was finished. The reason for that is his love of the competition, which for most of us was like blood to a shark.

Basketball only occupied so many hours in our time together, but we had to have something to do, and that something often involved competition of some sort.

I think someone invented playing cards to pass the time in airline terminals and on airplanes. We played waiting for takeoffs, we played while we were in the air, we played as we landed.

Tonk was the big card game, although every now and then we would play blackjack. Tonk was for Michael, Scottie, Ron Harper, and Jack Haley when he was with the team.

There was almost always a game going on in the back of the plane. There wasn't a regular winner. The money would go back and forth. Michael was the worst loser, and somehow he got worse depending on who beat him. He hated when Jack Haley won money from him.

I remember one time that I played and I won $150 off of Michael. The next trip, he wouldn't let me play. Then the next time out, Ron Harper was injured, so Michael let me play. He won his money back, and he said we were even. Then he wouldn't let me play ever again.

Steve, Luc, Jud, Dickey and I played blackjack from time to time. Every once in a while, we would get cerebral and play chess or backgammon, but that didn't last long.

We used to compete driving home from the airport. It's not like we would know who got home first, but we always made sure to honk when we passed each other on the highway home.

Golf, shooting jumpers in practice, even sometimes running laps or running lines, we would compete to see who would win. I don't know if that is the way it is on other teams, but it was part of our makeup. You can draw your own conclusions about whether that competitive nature helped us on the basketball floor.

Plane Rides

In the early 1990s, most teams took to taking charter plane rides, which was so much better than when we flew commercial. I know it sounds elitist, and it is, but the commercial flights were a pain for us for a number of reasons. There were fans to deal with, cramped seats for us big guys, even if we were in first class, flight delays, and we usually had to stay in town after a road game and get up early to fly home in the morning, rather than jumping on a charter flight home immediately after a game.

Those charter flights home after games were the most relaxing time for the team. We usually had decent food, we had terrific seating arrangements with a lot of room, and there was a real sense of being a team in a relaxing atmosphere. There wasn't a lot of craziness. A couple of times we took pictures of guys who were really ugly when they were sleeping, but for the most part it was just a bonding time.

You could watch movies on the monitors on the plane, and some guys had their own DVD players or laptop computers to watch movies. Some guys read books or magazines, some guys talked.

We usually fell into the same pairs or groups. There was Michael's group in the back of the plane, and I usually sat with Jud, Steve or Luc. Dennis usually sat by himself most of the time. He would watch the plane's monitor for a while, but he usually fell asleep. He needed his sleep, because he usually liked to go out on the town once we landed, no matter how late it was.

CHAPTER THIRTEEN

The All-Star Weekend and Michael's Return

Going for Three

Once we all got accustomed to the slam-dunk contest, the most exciting part of the annual NBA All-Star Game was the three-point shooting competition. Steve Kerr, my teammate and friend, participated in the shootout four years in a row, and finally won the event at the 1997 weekend in Cleveland.

When the All-Star weekend started out, it had the three-point shootout, the slam-dunk contest and an old-timers game. The old-timers were replaced by a rookie versus sophomore (or second-year player) game, and the slam dunk contest got to be such old hat that the league has trouble every year finding contestants. But the three-point contest is still the exact same competition it was at the start, and it remains the most entertaining part of the entire weekend, including the All-Star Game itself.

The Bulls had a significant history in the three-point shootout. Craig Hodges, a backup shooting guard with the first three championship teams, won the event in 1990, 1991, and 1992, and in 1991, hit 19 shots in a row. Steve Kerr was the next Bull to get involved, and he eventually succeeded.

Like everything else in his basketball life, Steve took the shootout seriously, although it was hard for us to find time to get him the practice he needed. We tried, though.

Once it got close to the All-Star weekend in February, a bunch of us—Jud, Luc and myself mainly—would set up the balls and the racks to help him get ready. The shootout required five racks and 25 balls, and we didn't have that many of either at the Berto Center, so we really had to hustle to simulate the event for Steve's benefit. We were running around, collecting balls, setting up racks, and trying to stay out of Steve's way, all in the minute alloted.

Steve wanted to win, and he got more involved every year that he did not win. I'm glad he got the victory in 1997, because he deserved it. When he left the Bulls, he was still the league's all-time leader in three-point shooting.

And Then There Was Michael

After recreating the Slam-Dunk competition in his own image, winning the event in 1987 and 1988, Michael Jordan got bored with the contest. But the league wanted his name attached to the All-Star Game Saturday activities, so it talked Michael into participating in the three-point shootout in 1990. Michael didn't have the best percentage in the league going in, but he did hit his fair share of three-pointers, and he was a competitor. It figured having him in the contest would make things interesting.

But Michael suffered one of his greatest embarrassments in NBA history when he finished last in the eight-man contest. He just wasn't hitting that day, and it happened to be with everyone watching.

I know this sounds mean, but I wish I was there for that.

I'm sure Michael took his fair share of ribbing for that performance, and the one thing I can say about Michael is that he was able to take that kind of abuse from friends and teammates if it was warranted.

And there was no escaping that one.

Berto Center

In 1992, the Bulls moved into the Sheri L. Berto Center in the northern suburb of Deerfield, Illinois. At the time, it was the premier training facility for any team in the league, and it remains one of the best buildings dedicated to one franchise.

Life at the Berto Center was pretty nice, although we didn't use it the way it might have been used by a team with younger players. Most of us had established home lives that we were quick to return to on practice days, so we didn't do as much hanging around as we might have in our younger days.

Most guys would come in and get their work done, then leave. It was a workplace, and loitering wasn't a team-endorsed activity.

But it was our locker room, our weight-lifting room, our pool. When we were there, we all seemed to relate to each other well. There was always a lot of noise, a lot of talking going on.

The gathering place was the training room, where we got wrapped or treated for our various physical ailments. The training room, where Chip Schaefer did his work, was the equivalent of a kitchen in the house, where we would all congregate to discuss the day's events.

There were times when other teams from the NBA, or college teams, or club teams, would use our facility for training, and they could not believe how nice we had it. I know that a couple of training facilities have been built in the last few years that had the Berto Center in mind, with the same general scheme.

The Picture

We had our players entrance to the Berto Center, but the more public face of the building was the front entrance. After the first door brought you into a small lobby, there was a second door that led to the basketball area.

A third door actually opened into a small hallway, with the basketball floor to the left and the weight room and locker rooms to the right. On the wall facing the door was a blown-up photograph from the 1991-92 season, the year the Bulls were chasing their second title. It covered the entire wall.

The picture was taken of several hundred fans standing and cheering the team on in a playoff game that took place at the Chicago Stadium, the former home of the Bulls. Among the many faces (faces we have all memorized over time), there was a woman holding a sign that read "We will defend what is ours."

While the picture has taken its share of criticism, simply because it is so big and the faces are so large and the expressions are so wild, we always took the message in that woman's sign seriously.

The players today might not fully understand what those words represent, because they no longer have anything to defend. After 1998, the Bulls' fortunes fell apart on the basketball floor, and some of the tradition fell apart as well.

But that picture, and the sign's message, seems timeless. That picture could be placed anywhere, in any era, and it would mean something.

Taping Before Games

Almost everybody in the NBA had his ankles taped before a game. The job fell to the trainer or a trainer's assistant to make our sometimes very ugly feet and ankles ready for the rigors of a 48-minute game of running and jumping.

When I was with the Bulls, there was no set order as to who would get taped first. But it was understood that if a veteran player was ready to get taped and a younger player was on the table waiting for attention, the older player got to be taped first and the young guy would have to wait for an opening.

With rookies, it's amazing they ever got taped at all. Some rookies would have to get in extra early to get taped beause otherwise they ran the risk of being bumped endlessly.

Things changed from the time I entered the league. There was so much more going on in the training room then just getting taped. Guys were undergoing other treatments, like ultra-sound, electro-stimulation, applied heat or applied ice. Again, those were treatments that required extra time, and anyone needing those treatments had to get to the game early.

On the road, it was fairly hectic, because we all got to the visiting stadium at the same time. Chip Schaefer and equipment manager John Ligmanowski had their hands full getting us ready on the road.

It's a shame fans can't see what it is like in the locker room after a regular season game. All anybody cared for was ice. It was for our knees.

The jumping and running we do in games, and the size of our bodies, caused particular damage to our knees. Everybody suffered from tendinitis, and the best treatment for tendinitis after a game was placing a plastic bag filled with ice on the knee. So all of us old guys would sit and ice our knees, talk about who got embarrassed, who made the best play. If it was after practice, we would discuss the rest of our day, whether we would get in a round of golf or see what our kids were up to.

But all we were really doing was trying to get our knees to stop burning.

Going to the Movies

Oh my gosh, did we watch a lot of videotape. And when it came time for the playoffs, we watched even more.

It was boring and often repetitive, but Phil kept it lively by inserting occasional snippets from hit movies. Sometimes the film clips were meant for comic relief, and sometimes they were meant to send a message. Sometimes, we didn't get the message, but that wasn't Phil's fault.

We saw *Full Metal Jacket* early on in my Bulls career. Johnny Bach, the longtime assistant coach with a military background, liked that movie.

One year, we saw the movie *What about Bob?* starring Richard Dreyfuss and Bill Murray. It took us a while to get the message there, although we realized it was all about taking baby steps on the way to your goal.

Another year, we saw the movie *Friday* starring Ice Cube. That one stumped us for a long time. Finally, we decided it was about being ourselves and doing what is right and getting through the hard times.

I never did fully understand why we saw *Pulp Fiction*. I think it was about how random events can affect your life, and trying to make meaning out of the randomness. Maybe it was about not eating too many quarter pounders, or trying not to say "What?'" all the time.

By the time the playoffs were over each year, we would have seen the entire film that was selected for that year's message.

Free Throws

Anyone who has ever played basketball in a team situation knows how coaches feel about free throws. It's the most important part of the game. For those teams that want to win, that's what they will tell you.

I would be shooting free throws after practice and think, "I wonder how many free throws I have shot in my life?" In all of my years of basketball, I don't know if I ever had a practice end with something other than shooting free throws.

On the championship Bulls, Steve Kerr was clearly the best free throw shooter. Michael got to be very good at them by the time he was done. We had a lot of guys who were hit and miss. Scottie, Luc, Ron, Toni, they were guys who should have been able to hit for a better percentage but just didn't. Unless you had a rhythm and a pattern to your approach, free throws could be very hard to make on a consistent basis.

Dennis Rodman had a unique approach to free throws. He hated them. He would tell you he didn't understand them. He didn't want to be at the line. At the line, he couldn't make a rebound, couldn't make a key defensive stand. Free throws slowed the game down, and Dennis didn't like that. So he would often just throw the ball up there, like you would throw a wadded up piece of paper at the waste paper basket.

But what was weird about Dennis was that he was really a good free throw shooter when he put his mind to it.

I remember one year when Don Nelson was coaching the Mavericks, and he decided the way to beat the Bulls was to foul Dennis consistently. It was similar to the tactic he used against Shaquille O'Neal, who was a notoriously poor free throw shooter. So Nelson has somebody foul Dennis routinely, and Dennis made nine out of 10, all at the end of the game. It became a matter of pride, and when Dennis cared about it, he turned out to be a good free throw shooter.

We would always end our practices with free throw shooting. Phil wanted us to make 10 in a row, which would signal the end of practice, and that put pressure on us to make one for the team.

We usually shot free throws in groups of three, with six baskets bordering the floor at the Berto Center. There would always be a competition between the three guys at each basket, with the winner being the first guy to make 10. Sometimes we played Bigs against Littles in free throw shooting. Even though we were closer to the basket, the little guys usually won that competition.

Defense

We had the most spectacular offensive player in the world in Michael Jordan. We had the best rebounder, perhaps ever, in Dennis Rodman. But I think our team defense was why we won games.

Our offense, the triangle, devised by assistant coach Tex Winter, received a lot of attention, because it was unusual, and it required so much study, and only the Bulls could run it with any efficiency and success. But all of the messages we received in practice, all of the attention given in team meetings, was about our defense.

We spent so much time on other teams' offensive principles, how to cover pick and rolls, executing different traps. With Michael, Scottie and Dennis, we had three guys who could cover a lot of ground very quickly. They made up for a lot of mistakes that we made, and gave the rest of us the opportunity to overplay on defense, knowing that we were covered if something went wrong.

Another thing that helped was that, just like with our offense, we players bought into the defensive principle. We were willing to put out the effort necessary, and that is such a big part of defense, just being willing to put out the effort.

I don't want to forget the contributions on defense from Ron Harper, who was a great fill-in for Michael on both ends of the floor. He used his long body very well. He knew how to play the angles to his benefit, and he had his reach and quickness to use to his advantage. He did a great job with that.

In the middle, I was certainly a different defensive presence than Luc Longley, who had that big body and took up a lot of space. I had to use my feet more and shift my body more than Luc did. I wasn't going to be strong enough to hold guys like Shaquille O'Neal out of the middle, so I had to junk it up a little bit more. I was able to help out on the weak side a little bit better because I was quicker.

For the first three-peat, the Bulls had assistant coach Johnny Bach, who was considered the defensive genius of the team. I got to spend one year under Johnny's tutelage, in 1993, before he left the team.

Johnny Bach prided himself on our defense, and that pride kind of caught on to everyone. We took our defense seriously. We would go into a game knowing what our opponent's scoring average was, and if we could hold that team under its average, then we had done our job. That was one statistic that was in our heads for almost every game.

When Johnny Bach left, Jim Cleamons did a lot of our defensive instruction. Phil also prided himself on being a strong defensive coach.

Stuff that Comes with Winning

As you grow up, coaches will tell you that playing well is its own reward, and that winning is just a byproduct of that. But winning is a pretty good reward for hard work, too.

When you win an NBA championship, you get lots of attention. You also get stuff, things the team and the league give you to commemorate your achievement. Hats and T-shirts are issued immediately, and you always wonder how the league has those things printed up ahead of time, when the outcome of the series is still in doubt. I wonder if there are championship hats and T-shirts for the Seattle SuperSonics or Utah Jazz from those finals we were in.

One thing you definitely get when you win an NBA championship is a championship ring. These are usually diamond-laden pieces of furniture you are supposed to wear on your hand, assuming you are strong enough to do so.

My first ring, the one from 1996, is my favorite. It's the most classic-looking ring of the bunch. It has a black face with 72 diamonds around it, signifying the fact we won a league-record 72 games that year. Inside the black are four NBA championship trophies, because it was the Bulls' fourth championship in six seasons.

It says "World Champion" on it, and also your name. You could actually wear it around, if you wanted to really call attention to who you were.

We received the rings in our first home game the following season.

The other two championship rings were really big and really shiny. One has our Bulls head logo on the top of it. The other had a big trophy with five smaller trophies inside of it, signifying the six titles. The Bull head ring had diamonds for its nose and horns.

These were rings no one would actually wear. They are too gaudy, although I guess that is the idea.

I hear that the championship rings have gotten even more extensive since we stopped winning. I can't imagine how much more flashy a ring could get.

Some people wear them a lot. I see some of the Bulls' employees from that era wearing them to work. Everyone asks to see them if they come by the house. I never wear mine, but everywhere I go people want to know why I don't.

I tell them they produce carpal-tunnel syndrome in the wrist from the great weight.

Other Stuff

Do you remember when the Bulls won the titles in 1991, 1992, and 1993, each year there was a really cool Wheaties box produced to commemorate the titles? We didn't get that.

There was one Wheaties box for our team, but there was never any real team picture on it. Michael didn't want to do it, so we didn't do it as a team. Steve and Luc looked into it, and I think it ended up having all of our team information on it with a picture of just Steve and Luc. It was a keeper.

We did receive a banner, the kind they hang from the street lights in the city of Chicago. They are big canvas banners, and I have three of those, one for each title. The one for 1995-96 was red, and it reads "Chicago Bulls, forever champions" on it, with all the players names listed.

For 1996-97, it lists all five championship teams. The last one, for 1997-98, reads "Incredi-Bull, Unbelieva-Bull, Unbeata-Bull, Unstoppa-Bull, Undenia-Bull, Unforgetta-Bull. 1997-98 Chicago Bulls, NBA World Champions.

In 1997, we got a humidor for our rings, which was a nice gift. In 1998, we got a glass box to display our rings in.

Each year we got home and away game-worn jerseys, which have value for souvenir collectors.

After the 1998 season, the Bulls were broken up and scattered to the four winds. I remember Scottie got his ring while playing with the Houston Rockets, and Steve Kerr got his when he came back to Chicago as a member of the San Antonio Spurs. That was a sad time, actually.

Keeping Michael's Secret

In the spring of 1995, we all knew Michael Jordan was coming back to play after his first retirement. It was the big secret we all had to keep.

Early in 1995, Michael had come back and practiced with us a couple of times, but it was more like when a big star returns to the TV show where he got his start. It was something to write about, something to talk about, but it wasn't about his comeback. It didn't feel that way. It was just two days, two practices, and they were on consecutive days. There wasn't any real indication that he was thinking about coming back.

About three weeks before his official announcement that he was coming back, he showed up at the Berto Center for practice. Only this time, he was in really good shape. And he was pushing himself.

The first day, we didn't think anything about it. He had shown up before. The second day, we starting thinking something was up. He was playing really hard, and he was taking part in all of our drills. The first time he came back, all he did was scrimmage with us.

This time, he did all the layup drills, all the defensive drills. It was clearly different, but it still felt like a guy trying to recapture something he had lost from a year and a half off.

He missed a day or two, and we stopped thinking about his return again. Then he came back and he stayed, for two weeks.

You didn't need to be a rocket scientist to see he was up to something. I think he was pushing himself to see what he could do, if his body was going to respond as he wanted it to. I guess he liked it, because he decided to make his return.

After one week of consistent practices, we kind of knew what was going on, but absolutely nobody asked him, "Are you coming back?" I don't know if we were afraid to jinx it, or we didn't want to fall into the trap Michael was setting for us.

The way he was working, we knew he was getting in shape for something, and we all started to believe that our dreams of playing with Michael Jordan were going to come true. Everybody's imagination started to run away. We were thinking, "If he comes back, we can be really good again." We were already one of the better teams in the East, and we were going to the playoffs, but this was a different possibility altogether.

There was no team meeting in which Michael told us he was coming back to the team. In fact, when it happened officially, there was no announcement made to the team. We just got to work.

I guess the team realized a big deal was going to be made of the decision, no matter what he did or we did to acknowledge it. So we just kept it under wraps as long as we could, and that was probably the least distractive way of doing it.

Do you remember how he told the world? He sent out faxes to the media, a simple piece of white paper that read "I'm back." That's how we all found out it was happening for real.

Michael returned to a team that was entirely different than the one he left. There was basically Scottie, and a bunch of guys he had never played with. Those of us who were new to the experience were aware that our dreams were coming true. It was the reason I joined the Bulls, the reason Steve was there, the reason Toni was with us. We were excited about the possibilities and I think we figured the sky is the limit. In hindsight, maybe we were a little overzealous that first spring, but we got our payoff the following three seasons.

Michael played 13 games at the end of the 1995 season, and there was an adjustment period. We did not play well in those 13 games, and we did not play well in the playoffs, getting eliminated in the Eastern Conference semifinals by the Orlando Magic. It turned out to be an embarrassing series for Michael, which may be why he came back with such a vengeance the next fall.

Celebrate the Heroes of Chicago and Illinois
in These Other Releases from Sports Publishing!